pathfinder guide

Somerset, Wiltshire *and* the Mendips

WALKS

Compiled by
Brian Conduit

D1318840

JARROLD

Ordnance Survey

Acknowledgements
The author is grateful for the invaluable advice and assistance
that he received from Somerset and Wiltshire County
Councils, and in particular to Les Davies, Mendip Hills
Warden, for his help on Black Down.

Text:	Brian Conduit
Photography:	Brian Conduit and
	Jarrold Publishing
Editors:	Richard Crowest, Donald Greig
Designers:	Brian Skinner, Doug Whitworth
Mapping:	Heather Pearson, Sandy Sims

Series Consultant: Brian Conduit

© Jarrold Publishing and Ordnance Survey 1997
Maps © Crown copyright 1997. The mapping in this guide is
based upon Ordnance Survey ® Pathfinder ®, Outdoor
Leisure ™, Explorer ™ and Travelmaster ® mapping. Ordnance
Survey, Pathfinder and Travelmaster are registered trade
marks and Outdoor Leisure and Explorer are trade marks of
Ordnance Survey, the National Mapping Agency of Great
Britain.

Jarrold Publishing   ISBN 0-7117-0877-0

While every care has been taken to ensure the accuracy of the
route directions, the publishers cannot accept responsibility
for errors or omissions, or for changes in details given. The
countryside is not static: hedges and fences can be removed,
field boundaries can alter, footpaths can be rerouted and
changes in ownership can result in the closure or diversion of
some concessionary paths. Also, paths that are easy and
pleasant for walking in fine conditions may become slippery,
muddy and difficult in wet weather, while stepping stones
across rivers and streams may become impassable.

 If you find an inaccuracy in either the text or maps, please
write to Jarrold Publishing or Ordnance Survey respectively at
one of the addresses below.

First published 1997
by Jarrold Publishing and Ordnance Survey

Printed in Great Britain
by Jarrold Book Printing, Thetford, Norfolk 1/97

Jarrold Publishing,
Whitefriars, Norwich NR3 1TR
Ordnance Survey,
Romsey Road, Southampton SO16 4GU

Front cover:	Glastonbury Tor
Previous page:	Stonehenge

Contents

Short, easy walks

Walks of modest
length, likely to
involve some
modest uphill
walking

More challenging
walks which may
be longer and/or
over more rugged
terrain, often with
some stiff climbs

OF THE SEVERN

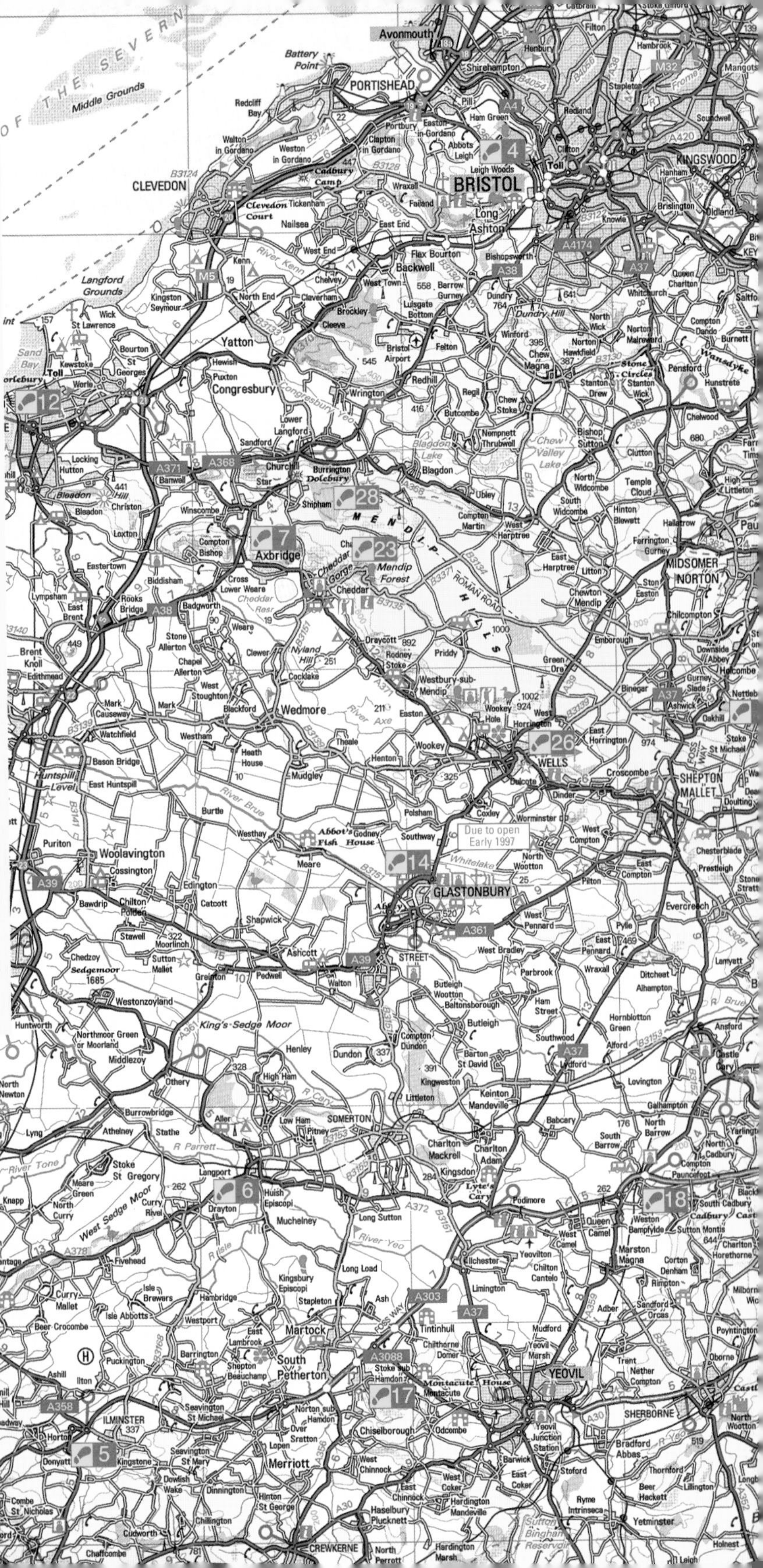

Middle Grounds

Battery Point

Avonmouth

PORTISHEAD

BRISTOL

KINGSWOOD

CLEVEDON

Long Ashton

Leigh Woods

Yatton

Congresbury

Langford Grounds

Axbridge

Cheddar

MENDIP HILLS

Mendip Forest

Wedmore

Woolavington

WELLS

SHEPTON MALLET

MIDSOMER NORTON

GLASTONBURY

STREET

King's Sedge Moor

West Sedge Moor

Sedgemoor

Westonzoyland

SOMERTON

Langport

Muchelney

Long Sutton

Martock

South Petherton

ILMINSTER

YEOVIL

SHERBORNE

Montacute House

CREWKERNE

Merriott

Bristol Airport

Chew Valley Lake

Blagdon Lake

Sutton Bingham Reservoir

SCALE 1:312 500 or 1 INCH to 5 MILES *1CM to 3.1 KM*

0 2 4 6 8 10 KILOMETRES 15

0 2 4 MILES 8 10

KEYMAP HEIGHTS SHOWN IN FEET

SCALE 1:312 500 or 1 INCH to 5 MILES *1CM to 3.1 KM*

KILOMETRES
0   2   4   6   8   10   15

MILES
0   2   4   6   8   10

KEYMAP HEIGHTS SHOWN IN FEET

CHIPPING SODBURY
YATE
BATH
AQUAE SVLIS
CHIPPENHAM
CALNE
MELKSHAM
DEVIZES
BRADFORD-ON-AVON
TROWBRIDGE
WESTBURY
WARMINSTER
FROME
MERE
WINCANTON
GILLINGHAM
SHAFTESBURY
Bruton

Keymap 2

At-a-glance...

Walk	Page	Start	Distance	Time
Avebury, West Kennett and Silbury Hill	40	Avebury	6½ miles (10.5km)	3 hrs
Axbridge and Cheddar Reservoir	26	Axbridge	5 miles (8km)	2½ hrs
Barbury Castle and Ogbourne St Andrew	77	Barbury Castle Country Park	8½ miles (13.7km)	4 hrs
Bradford-on-Avon, Westwood and Avoncliff	60	Bradford-on-Avon	7 miles (11.3km)	3½ hrs
Burrington Combe, Dolebury Warren and Black Down	87	Burrington Combe	8½ miles (13.7km)	4½ hrs
Cadbury Castle and the Corton Ridge	54	Cadbury Castle	6½ miles (10.5km)	3 hrs
Cheddar Gorge	70	Cheddar	5 miles (8km)	3 hrs
Devizes and Caen Hill Locks	18	Devizes, the Wharf Centre	4 miles (6.4km)	2 hrs
Fovant Down	34	Fovant, by the church	4½ miles (7.2km)	2 hrs
Glastonbury	43	Glastonbury	6½ miles (10.5km)	3½ hrs
Ham Hill, Montacute and Norton Sub Hamdon	51	Ham Hill Country Park	6 miles (9.7km)	3 hrs
Hinton Charterhouse and Wellow	57	Off the A36 between Bath and Warminster	7 miles (11.3km)	3½ hrs
Ilminster and Herne Hill	22	Ilminster	3½ miles (5.6km)	2 hrs
Lacock and Bowden Park	31	Lacock, on the edge of the village	6½ miles (10.5km)	3½ hrs
Lambourn Downs	46	Lambourn	7 miles (11.3km)	3 hrs
Langport and Muchelney Abbey	24	Langport, Cocklemoor car park	5 miles (8km)	2½ hrs
Leigh Woods and the Avon Gorge	20	Leigh Woods car park	3½ miles (5.6km)	2 hrs
Nettlebridge and Harridge Wood	16	Nettlebridge	3½ miles (5.6km)	2 hrs
Nunney Combe	14	Nunney	3½ miles (5.6km)	2 hrs
Old and New Wardour Castles	36	Old Wardour Castle	4 miles (6.4km)	2 hrs
Pewsey Downs	64	Walkers Hill	7 miles (11.3km)	3½ hrs
Salisbury and Old Sarum	28	Salisbury	5½ miles (8.9km)	2½ hrs
Savernake Forest	83	Marlborough	10 miles (16.1km)	5 hrs
Stonehenge	67	Amesbury	8 miles (12.9km)	4 hrs
Tollard Royal and Win Green	73	Tollard Royal	7 miles (11.3km)	3½ hrs
Uffington Monuments and Vale of the White Horse	48	National Trust car park on Whitehorse Hill	6½ miles (10.5km)	3 hrs
Wells, Ebbor Gorge and Wookey Hole	80	Wells	7½ miles (12.1km)	4 hrs
Weston Woods and Sand Bay	38	Sand Bay car park	6 miles (9.7km)	3 hrs

Comments

A fascinating walk on the Marlborough Downs, taking in the finest collection of prehistoric monuments in the country.

There are views of the Mendips and across the Somerset Levels from this attractive walk that partially encircles Cheddar reservoir.

From an Iron Age hillfort high up on the Marlborough Downs, the route follows the Ridgeway down into the valley below and then climbs back on to the downs.

There are several hilly sections, but in between much pleasant and relaxing walking by the rivers Avon and Frome and the Kennet and Avon Canal.

The walk leads through woodland and across heathland on to Black Down to reach the highest point on the Mendips. The views from there are superb.

There are magnificent views from both the Corton ridge and Cadbury Castle, alleged site of King Arthur's court of Camelot.

The final stage of this energetic walk, along the rim of Cheddar Gorge, is particularly spectacular and memorable.

Whether or not you are a canal enthusiast, there is much of interest at the Wharf Centre in Devizes and when descending the Caen Hill flight of locks.

Fovant churchyard and the regimental badges carved on the side of Fovant Down are reminders of the 1914-18 war. There are fine views from the top of the down.

Most of the historic and mythical sites around Glastonbury are linked by this walk, finishing with a climb to the grand viewpoint of Glastonbury Tor.

Chief ingredients of this walk are several grand viewpoints, beautiful woodland, two attractive villages and the chance to visit an Elizabethan mansion.

The walk passes through two villages and there are many fine views over the eastern Mendips.

From the wooded slopes of Herne Hill, there are fine views over Ilminster and the Isle valley.

An attractive but fairly tortuous route, with superb views over the Avon valley and the chance to explore a picturesque village and visit an interesting country house.

Enjoy spaciousness and extensive views across the Berkshire Downs on this walk in horse racing country.

An easy but highly atmospheric walk across part of the Somerset Levels and by the River Parrett, with a visit to a ruined abbey.

A walk through attractive woodland is followed by spectacular views of the Avon gorge and Clifton Suspension Bridge.

A secluded valley and quiet woodlands disguise that in Victorian times this was a thriving industrial area.

A beautiful short walk through a wooded combe, with a medieval castle to explore at the end.

You pass through landscaped parkland and woodland on a walk that links a ruined medieval castle with its 18th-century successor.

You enjoy some fine downland walking, grand views over the Vale of Pewsey, two ancient churches and an attractive stretch of the Kennet and Avon Canal.

A fascinating historic walk, much of it beside the River Avon, linking Salisbury with its now deserted predecessor.

Most of this lengthy walk is through the woodlands and along the grand beech-lined avenues of a former royal forest.

The most memorable part of this thoroughly absorbing walk is the approach to Stonehenge across the wide expanses of Salisbury Plain.

There are superb and extensive views both from Win Green, the highest point on Cranborne Chase, and the subsequent ridge top path.

This modest walk not only visits three major prehistoric sites but also includes a picturesque village and magnificent views over the Vale of the White Horse.

A steady climb on to the Mendip plateau is followed by a descent of Ebbor Gorge. You pass the caves at Wookey Hole and there are grand views of Wells Cathedral on the final stretch.

Much of the walk is along a thickly wooded ridge to the north of Weston-super-Mare and there are some splendid sea views.

At-a-glance...

Introduction to Somerset, Wiltshire and The Mendips

Both scenically and historically Somerset and Wiltshire must rank as two of the most attractive and interesting counties in the country. Landscapes range from the breezy heights of the Mendips to the flat, watery meadows of the Somerset Levels, and from the rolling chalk uplands of the Marlborough Downs to the mudflats and sandy expanses that fringe the Bristol Channel coast. The variety of sites of historic interest is even greater. What other region can rival the boast of Europe's greatest concentration – and most impressive examples – of prehistoric monuments; two of England's loveliest cathedrals and most attractive cathedral cities; one of the most elegant and dramatic of suspension bridges; plus a fair sprinkling of castles, abbeys and stately homes? This region, where history, myth and legend have become inseparably linked, may have seen the beginnings of Christianity in Britain and was the heartland of both Arthur's kingdom and Alfred the Great's Wessex.

This walking guide does not coincide with the exact boundaries of Somerset and Wiltshire. Exmoor and the Quantock Hills in west Somerset are excluded as they are already covered in another title in the series. But as the North Wessex Downs – the collective name for that great swathe of chalk uplands that sweep across Wiltshire – extend eastwards into neighbouring Berkshire and Oxfordshire, two walks have been included just across the borders of those counties.

Somerset means 'summer pastures' and gets its name from the blue lias town of Somerton, once a place of some importance but now a sleepy though attractive backwater. Stretching across the north of the county from the coastal lowlands in the west and descending to the Frome valley and Wiltshire border in the east are the Mendips, a range of broad-backed limestone hills. Here is a classic carboniferous limestone landscape of crags, rocky outcrops, deep gorges, caves and waterfalls. Every year thousands come to marvel at the spectacular deep gash of Cheddar Gorge and the highly popular caves at its base, but there are others. To the north is Burrington Combe, situated below the highest point on the Mendips on Black Down (1067ft/325m). To the south-east is the Ebbor Gorge, which many claim to be the most attractive of all, partly because it is the only one that does not have a road running through it.

To the north the Mendips overlook Bristol, Bath and the River Avon, which flows through another world famous gorge at Clifton; here a natural wonder is spanned by a man-made wonder, Brunel's great suspension bridge. To the south they descend abruptly to the beautiful cathedral city of Wells and the lowlands of the Somerset Levels, one of the most

Ham Hill

atmospheric and distinctive landscapes in the country and still subject to winter flooding. Above the surrounding wetlands rise low hills, such as the Poldens, and a number of islands or moors on which the main settlements grew up; Athelney, Muchelney and above all the legendary Isle of Avalon. Here stands Glastonbury, seat of the largest and richest monastery in medieval England and centre of a myriad of ancient myths and legends. Was it here that Joseph of Arimathea founded the first Christian site in the country? Is the Holy Grail buried here? Are the graves by the transepts of the ruined abbey really those of Arthur and Guinevere? These legends drew medieval pilgrims to Glastonbury and still attract a wide mix of tourists today. Brooding over the whole scene is the mysterious, conical-shaped Glastonbury Tor on which the last abbot was hanged in 1539.

As well as legends, the Somerset Levels have rather more tangible associations with great historic events. It was here that Alfred the Great retreated after his defeat by the Danes, where he is alleged to have burnt the cakes, and where he signed a treaty with his Danish enemies at Wedmore in 878. Eight centuries later the last battle on English soil was fought here at Sedgemoor in 1685, when James II defeated the Duke of Monmouth's attempt to seize his throne.

The ruins of Glastonbury Abbey

Beyond the levels the land rises again towards the Dorset border. This is warm, honey-coloured hamstone country with picturesque villages, attractive market towns and a number of great country houses. Here is another link with the Arthurian legends, the hillfort of Cadbury Castle, claimed as the site of the king's court of Camelot.

Eastwards is Wiltshire, a county which, like Somerset, takes its name from a once major town – Wilton – that has declined and been superseded by others. The fringes of the Cotswolds clip the north-west of the county and to the east and south of the hills, in the valley of the Bristol Avon, are lovely limestone towns and villages, like Bradford-on-Avon and the National Trust village of Lacock, made wealthy by the profits of the medieval wool trade.

Beyond the Avon lie the great expanses of rolling chalk downs that dominate the landscape of much of Wiltshire. On the Marlborough Downs is the greatest concentration of prehistoric remains in the country, particularly around the great stone circle at Avebury where the West Kennett Long Barrow and Silbury Hill, the highest artificial mound in Europe, are among the sites within easy reach. The downs extend across the Berkshire and Oxfordshire borders to continue as the Berkshire Downs. Here another great prehistoric concentration is centred on the White Horse of Uffington. Traversing the ridge of these downs and linking many of the sites is the Ridgeway, one of the oldest routeways in Europe which is now put to good use as a National Trail.

To the south the Marlborough Downs descend to the beautiful Vale of Pewsey, through which runs the Kennet and Avon Canal, a newer routeway across the region, built in the early 19th century to provide a waterway link between London and Bristol. Here is the valley of the other River Avon, the Wiltshire or Hampshire Avon, which flows across Salisbury Plain. The plain – really a gently rolling plateau – occupies the heart of the county. Here is the most famous prehistoric monument of all – Stonehenge – situated on a low ridge in the centre of the plain, visible for miles around and also surrounded by numerous other ancient sites.

A track runs southwards from Stonehenge to Old Sarum, a deserted medieval city. In 1075 the Normans made it the seat of a bishop and within its walls a castle and cathedral were built. In 1220 it was abandoned after the bishop moved down into the valley below to found New Sarum – better known as Salisbury – on the banks of the Avon. This was a purpose-built city with a new cathedral, built in less than 40 years, which boasts the tallest spire in Britain.

In the south of Wiltshire, near the Hampshire and Dorset borders, stretch more chalk downs, the West Wiltshire Downs and Cranborne Chase, the latter shared with Dorset. This is a former hunting area and here the valleys that cut into the downs are more wooded. From the highest point on the chase at Win Green (911ft/277m) the views are magnificent and even extend to the Isle of Wight.

There are few other areas in the country where history and the landscape are so closely interwoven as in these two Wessex counties. With such a varied countryside and range of historic sites, plus lovely old towns and idyllic villages, attractive pubs and appealing tea shops, walking in Somerset and Wiltshire is a sheer joy. Whether you take to the hills or river valleys, downs or woodlands, coast or lowlands, the area is full of fascinating places to seek out.

Nunney Combe

Start	Nunney
Distance	3½ miles (5.6km)
Approximate time	2 hours
Parking	Roadside parking in Nunney
Refreshments	Pub at Nunney
Ordnance Survey maps	Landranger 183 (Yeovil & Frome), Explorer 5 (Mendip Hills East)

This short and easy walk takes you through gently rolling countryside on the eastern slopes of the Mendips. The first half of the route is mostly through the delightful, steep-sided Nunney Combe; the second half is across fields. Muddy conditions can be expected in places.

At Nunney it is the 13th- to 14th-century church, not the castle, that stands on high ground overlooking the attractive village. The reason is that the castle came much later, a small moated tower house, four storeys high, built in the late 14th century by Sir John Delamere. Never very powerful, it succumbed easily to Parliamentary forces after a brief siege in 1645.

Start in the Market Place, turn left to cross the bridge over Nunney Brook and follow the road uphill. At a small layby bear right on to a path which continues gently uphill, between bushes and trees, to a stile. Climb it and walk along the right edge of a field to climb another one.

A worn path bears right towards the field edge but the right of way lies straight ahead across the field. In front of a tree-lined embankment, turn right and by the field edge turn left to a stile. Climb it, cross a footbridge over Nunney Brook and turn left. Now follows a most attractive part of the

The ill-fated Nunney Castle

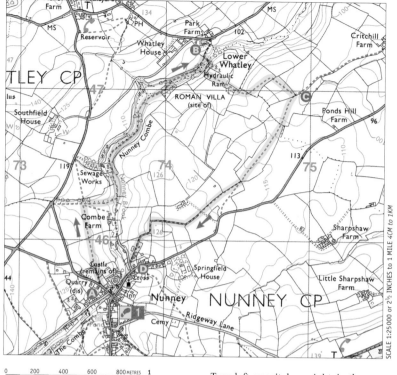

SCALE 1:25 000 or 2½ INCHES to 1 MILE 4CM to 1KM

```
0    200    400    600    800 METRES  1
                              KILOMETRES
                              MILES
0    200    400    600 YARDS   ½
```

walk as you keep beside the brook through the wooded, steep-sided Nunney Combe, carpeted with bluebells in spring. On reaching a track, turn left to cross a bridge over the brook. A few yards beyond, turn right over a stile, at a public footpath sign, to continue along the opposite bank through the combe. This path is likely to be muddy in places.

The path bears left away from the brook and heads up to a track. Turn right **B** to re-cross the brook and follow the track round a right-hand bend. Where the track enters a field, turn left through a waymarked metal gate, then continue across a field, keeping close to and parallel with its right edge, and go through a metal gate at the far end. Turn left and keep along the left edge of the next field, by a hedge on the left, in which you need to keep an eye out for a stile.

Turn left over it, bear right, in the direction of a waymark, and head diagonally across a field to a stile in the far corner. Climb it, walk along the left edge of the next field down to a stile, climb that one, turn half-right **C** and head across the next field, making for a stile. Climb it, and another one immediately in front, turn left along the field edge and shortly afterwards turn right, continuing along the left edge of the field. In the field corner, turn left over a stile and turn right to continue along the right edge of the next field. Climb a stile, cross a track, climb another one and keep along the right edge of a field, bearing right to a stile.

Climb it and continue along an enclosed, tree-lined path which, after following it around left and right bends and climbing another stile, widens out into a track. Head gently downhill to a lane and turn left down to the main street in Nunney **D**. Turn right and walk through the village, passing the old market cross, to return to the start.●

Nettlebridge And Harridge Wood

Start	Nettlebridge
Distance	3½ miles (5.6km)
Approximate time	2 hours
Parking	On verge near telephone box beside lane to the east of the A367 – park carefully as space is restricted
Refreshments	Pub on main road at Nettlebridge
Ordnance Survey maps	Landranger 183 (Yeovil & Frome), Explorer 5 (Mendip Hills East)

The undoubted highlight of this short and easy walk in the eastern Mendips is the middle section which takes you through a beautiful, steep-sided wooded valley along the lower edge of Harridge Wood, passing beside a stream and by rock faces. It is difficult to believe that in the 19th century this peaceful and remote area was the location for a paper mill and housed a busy industrial community. Parts of this route are likely to be muddy after wet weather.

Begin at the telephone box in the small and scattered hamlet of Nettlebridge. Go through a metal gate, at a public footpath sign, and walk along the right edge of a field to a stile. Climb it, bear slightly left across an uneven field, go

over a small rise and keep ahead to climb another stile. Continue across a field, go through a metal gate and on

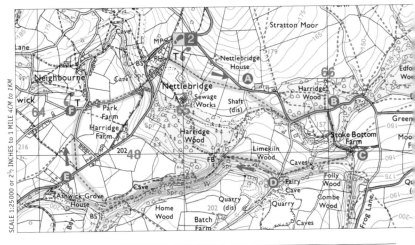

across the next field to where another metal gate leads you on to a lane.

Keep ahead but almost immediately turn right Ⓐ through a metal gate, bear left and walk diagonally across a field, skirting the corner of a wood and heading down to join an obvious path beside a brook. Climb a stile to rejoin the lane, keep ahead gently uphill and after ¼ mile (400m), turn right Ⓑ down the tarmac drive to Stoke Bottom Farm. Cross a stream, bear left towards the farm, go through the farmyard and turn right Ⓒ, between the house and farm buildings, to a metal gate.

Harridge Wood

Go through, turn right along the right edge of a field, passing behind the house, and continue by a hedge on the right, bearing left away from the field edge to pass through a gap to the left of two old gateposts. To the left is St Dunstan's Well, fed by a small stream, and nearby are several small caves. Continue along the right edge of a field, by a wire fence and trees on the right, and climb a stile on to a lane Ⓓ. Cross over and, at a public footpath sign to Shepton Mallet, go through a gate and head across a field, keeping parallel to the left edge. Later keep alongside the edge of trees, climb a stile to enter Harridge Wood and at a fork and footpath post to the left of a ruined cottage, take the left-hand path, in the direction of Oakhill.

Now follows a most attractive part of the walk as you continue through a steep-sided, wooded valley – almost a gorge – keeping by a stream on the right, passing limestone rock faces and at one point a waterfall. In spring the wood is carpeted with bluebells. At a three-way fork by a footpath post, take the right-hand uphill path (still in the Oakhill direction), by a wall on the left, which curves right to a stone stile. Climb it and head straight across a field to climb another one in the far left corner just to the right of a bungalow. Turn right Ⓔ along the road, almost immediately turn left over a stone stile, head diagonally across a field and climb another stone stile on to a lane.

Turn left and at a crossroads turn right Ⓕ, signposted No Through Road, along a very narrow lane which later descends steeply and rounds a right-hand bend to reach the main road. Turn left and after about 100 yds (91m), bear right downhill along an enclosed, tarmac path. The path later widens into a track and passes between houses to reach the starting point by the telephone box. ●

Devizes and Caen Hill Locks

Start	Devizes, the Wharf Centre
Distance	4 miles (6.4km)
Approximate time	2 hours
Parking	Wharf Centre at Devizes
Refreshments	Pubs and cafés in Devizes, café at Wharf Centre, pub by point Ⓐ
Ordnance Survey maps	Landranger 173 (Swindon & Devizes), Pathfinders 1184, ST86/96 (Melksham) and 1185, SU06/16 (Devizes & Marlborough)

This is essentially a canalside walk and its main feature is the impressive Caen Hill Flight of Locks, one of the major engineering triumphs of the canal age, by which the Kennet and Avon canal descends from the Vale of Pewsey to the Avon valley. Canal lovers will find much of interest at the Wharf Centre in Devizes and there are fine views over the Avon valley and downs.

The large, handsome Market Place is the main focal point of Devizes. The town boasts two medieval churches, both dating back to the 12th century; some fine Georgian houses; a Victorian brewery and a 19th-century castle built in the style of its Norman predecessor, on whose site it stands. By the canal, close to the town centre, is the attractively restored Wharf Centre. The two original buildings which survive now house a theatre and the headquarters of the Kennet and Avon Canal Trust – the latter, a former granary, has a shop and museum.

Facing the canal, turn right under the bridge, then sharp right up to the road and right again to cross the bridge. Turn left to join the canal towpath, turn left over the first road bridge, left again at a public footpath sign 'Caen Hill Locks via Subway', and then turn sharp left to pass under the bridge.

Continue along the other bank of the canal, passing several locks, go under

the next bridge (Prison Bridge) Ⓐ and keep ahead to reach the top of the Caen Hill Locks. This flight of 29 locks in just over 2 miles (3.25km) was built by John Rennie, the canal engineer, to overcome the problem of taking the canal up the

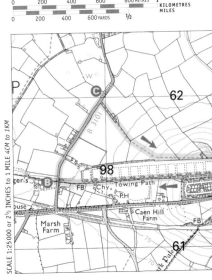

SCALE 1:25000 or 2½ INCHES to 1 MILE 4CM to 1KM

At the top of Caen Hill Locks

237ft (72m) rise from the Avon valley to Devizes. Sixteen of the locks were built close together down Caen Hill, a distance of only about $^1/_2$ mile (800m).

As you descend gently beside these 16 locks there are fine views ahead over the Avon valley. At the bottom of the flight go under a bridge **B** and immediately turn left up to a road. Turn sharp left to cross the bridge, continue along the road and at a parking sign for Caen Hill Locks and a public footpath sign 'Prison Bridge and Bath Road', turn right along a broad track **C**.

Follow the track gently uphill and at the parking area climb some steps and turn left along a broad, grassy track beside the Side Pounds. These square-shaped ponds were built to provide a steady supply of water to the locks. Climb a stile and continue along a track, later tree-lined, to emerge on to a road. Turn right to cross Prison Bridge, turn left **A** and descend steps, then turn right on to the towpath and retrace your steps to the start. ●

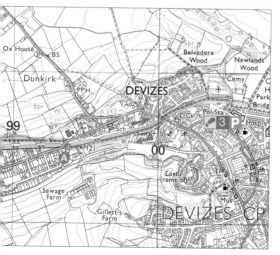

Leigh Woods and the Avon Gorge

Start	Forestry Commission's Leigh Woods car park, signposted from the A369 to the west of Clifton Suspension Bridge.
Distance	3½ miles (5.6km)
Approximate time	2 hours
Parking	Leigh Woods
Refreshments	None
Ordnance Survey maps	Landranger 172 (Bristol & Bath), Pathfinder 1166, ST47/57 (Portishead & Bristol (West))

The highlight of this short and easy walk is the middle section along the west side of the Avon gorge. From here there are dramatic views down the gorge to the Clifton Suspension Bridge. The first and last parts of the route take you through the very attractive Leigh Woods, parts of which form the Avon Gorge Nature Reserve.

Brunel's spectacular Clifton Suspension Bridge, over the equally spectacular Avon Gorge

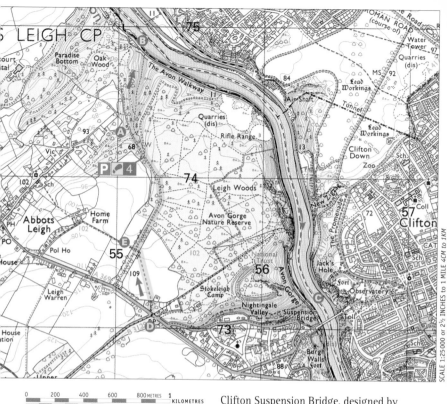

SCALE 1:25000 or 2½ INCHES to 1 MILE 4CM to 1KM

```
0    200   400   600   800 METRES  1
                                    KILOMETRES
                                    MILES
0    200   400   600 YARDS    ½
```

Start by turning left out of the car park and walk gently downhill along a tarmac forest drive, which soon becomes a straight track. Where this ends, turn right Ⓐ along a track and head down to a red and yellow topped marker post. Bear left to follow a broad track steadily downhill through woodland, ignoring a left turn at another red and yellow topped post. The track later narrows to a path, continues downhill and passes under a disused railway bridge to a T-junction of paths on the banks of the River Avon Ⓑ.

Turn right to join the Avon Walkway and follow it along the west side of the Avon gorge – a spectacular walk but also rather a noisy one because of the busy road that runs along the east side. The path, tree-lined at times, keeps below the steep cliffs and later gives grand views of the striking and graceful Clifton Suspension Bridge, designed by Brunel. Work on the bridge began in 1836 but it was not completed until 1864, five years after Brunel's death.

Just before reaching the bridge turn right Ⓒ at a public footpath sign, pass under another disused railway bridge and head steadily uphill through more fine woodland. Eventually the path turns left through a kissing gate on to a road by an 'Avon Gorge National Nature Reserve' notice. Turn right along the road to a T-junction, then turn right again along the main road to a junction with traffic lights Ⓓ.

Here turn right, at a public footpath sign, along a tarmac track which passes to the right of a bungalow. Climb a stile, turn half-left and head diagonally across a field towards another bungalow. Turn left at a fence corner to reach a stile, climb it and continue along a track to a tarmac drive. Turn right Ⓔ and follow the drive back to the car park. ●

Ilminster and Herne Hill

Start	Ilminster
Distance	3½ miles (5.6km)
Approximate time	2 hours
Parking	Ilminster
Refreshments	Pubs and cafés at Ilminster, pub at Donyatt
Ordnance Survey maps	Landranger 193 (Taunton & Lyme Regis), Pathfinder 1278, ST21/31 (Ilminster)

From Ilminster this short walk heads up over the attractive wooded slopes of Herne Hill, then descends into the valley of the River Isle to the village of Donyatt. The return leg takes a more low level route. There are fine views throughout, especially of the town, dominated by the tower of its imposing church.

Ilminster's church, the minster that gives its name to this pleasant and bustling south Somerset market town, is a large and impressive 15th-century building with a tall central tower that can be seen for miles around. The walk starts in the town centre in front of the old Market House.

Walk along Silver Street, in the Langport and Taunton direction, pass to the left of the church and turn left down Wharf Lane. At a T-junction, turn left **A**, then turn right along Orchard Vale, passing to the left of playing fields.

Head uphill through a new housing area and just where the road curves left near the top, turn right **B** on to a short section of road. Where this ends, keep ahead through a hedge gap and cross a narrow field – a disused railway track – into woodland to reach a junction of tracks. Go through a gate, in the Donyatt direction, and continue along a most attractive enclosed path which curves to the right and gives fine views

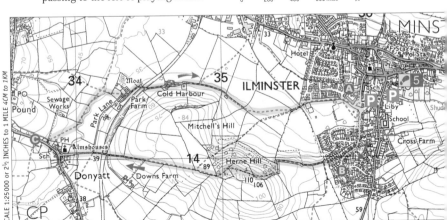

The route offers broad views of Ilminster

Turn right through the attractive village of warm-coloured hamstone cottages, many of them thatched. After the last of the thatched cottages, turn right along a tarmac track Ⓒ. Ahead are two metal gates: go through the right-hand one and immediately turn half-left to head diagonally across a field. Climb a half-hidden stile in the far corner and continue along the curving right-hand edge of the next field, with the river over to the right, bearing left to a metal gate. Go through and walk along the right edge of the next field, then turn right to cross a footbridge over the river.

over Ilminster and the Isle valley. Pass through a gap beside a gate, turn left to continue along the left inside edge of woodland and turn right to enter Herne Hill Woods.

At a fork immediately ahead take the left-hand upper path, then at the next fork take the left-hand path again, ascending steps and continuing uphill through the trees. At the top, pass to the right of a solitary picnic table and at a crossroads of paths, bear left downhill to a kissing gate. Go through, here emerging from the woods, walk along the left edge of a field and go through a metal gate. Ahead are extensive views across the Vale of Taunton looking towards the Black Down Hills.

Descend gently along the left edge of the next field, keep ahead to cross a track and continue along an enclosed downhill path to a lane. Keep ahead towards the picturesque village of Donyatt, crossing two bridges – the first over a disused railway and the second over the River Isle – then head up to a T-junction to the left of the 15th-century church.

Walk across the field ahead, pass between gateposts, bear left diagonally across the next field and go through a metal gate in the corner beside a barn. Keep ahead in front of cottages and turn left along a tarmac track. Follow it over the disused railway track again, through the buildings of Cold Harbour Farm, after which it reverts to a rough track. Where this ends at a metal gate and stile, climb the stile and bear left diagonally across a field to a metal kissing gate in the far corner. Continue along the path ahead, go through another kissing gate and follow a tarmac path to a road.

Bear right, then after a few yards enter playing fields and continue by a hedge along their left-hand edge, parallel to the road on the left. In the corner of the playing fields, turn left through a wooden barrier on to the road Ⓐ, then turn left again and immediately turn right along Wharf Lane to return to Ilminster town centre and the start. ●

Langport and Muchelney Abbey

Start	Langport, Cocklemoor car park
Distance	5 miles (8km)
Approximate time	2½ hours
Parking	Langport
Refreshments	Pubs and café at Langport, light refreshments at Muchelney Abbey
Ordnance Survey maps	Landranger 193 (Taunton & Lyme Regis), Pathfinder 1259, ST42/52 (Langport, Somerton & Ilchester)

This well-waymarked walk, ideal for a languid summer afternoon, is in the heart of the Somerset Levels, a highly distinctive area of low-lying pastures, slow moving rivers and distant views of tall church towers across flat meadows. Much of the route is beside the River Parrett and there is a short detour to the ruins of a medieval abbey. In winter or after rain, some of the riverside meadows may be partially flooded.

Originally an important river port, Langport's prosperity declined with the rise of Bridgwater downstream, but some vestiges of its former greatness remain. On the hill to the east of the town centre is one of the old town gates with the 'Hanging Chapel' above it, and nearby is the 15th-century church.

From the car park, which is signposted from the main street, take the path that leads off from the bottom end, by a rhyne or drainage channel on the left, to the riverbank. Turn left along it, climb a metal stile, cross a footbridge over the rhyne and follow an embankment above the River Parrett around a slow right-hand curve to Huish Bridge Ⓐ.

Turn right over it, walk along a track, cross a bridge over a rhyne and turn left to climb two waymarked stiles in quick succession. Bear right to descend an embankment, head diagonally across a field and climb a stile in the far corner. Turn left along an enclosed track, climb a stile, turn right over another and continue along the right edge of a field by a wire fence and line of trees. In the field corner

The River Parrett

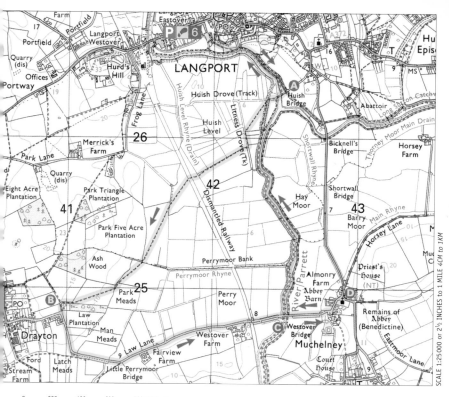

SCALE 1:25000 or 2½ INCHES to 1 MILE 4CM to 1KM

climb two stiles in quick succession, crossing the intervening rhyne, keep ahead across the next field, climb a stile, cross the track of a disused railway and go through the gate ahead.

Bear left, walk diagonally across the next three fields, climbing two stiles, and in the corner of the third field go through a metal gate. Bear left alongside a hedge on the right, looking out for where you turn right over a waymarked stile. Bear left diagonally across the next field and climb a stile in the far corner. Continue along an enclosed path and follow it around a left bend to emerge on to a road on the edge of Drayton **B**.

Keep along the road for just over 1 mile (1.6km) to Westover Bridge **C**. The route turns left just before the bridge but keep ahead over it into the village of Muchelney **D**, which is well

worth a short detour. Although there is not much left of the abbey except for the foundations, the trio of Benedictine abbey, 15th-century church and 14th-century thatched Priest's House makes an interesting grouping. The only part of the abbey above ground level is the impressive and largely intact 15th-century Abbot's Lodging.

Return to Westover Bridge **C**, cross it and turn right over a stile, at a public footpath sign to Huish Bridge. The next part of the walk is along an embankment above the lazily meandering River Parrett, over a series of stiles and with extensive views across the meadows. The three church towers that can be seen above the flat terrain are those of Langport, Huish Episcopi and Muchelney.

Finally bear left away from the river, keeping beside a rhyne on the right, and climb two stiles to reach a track. Turn right, cross Huish Bridge **A** and retrace your steps to the start.

Axbridge and Cheddar Reservoir

Start	Axbridge
Distance	5 miles (8km)
Approximate time	2½ hours
Parking	Axbridge
Refreshments	Pubs and cafés at Axbridge
Ordnance Survey maps	Landranger 182 (Weston-super-Mare & Bridgwater), Explorer 4 (Mendip Hills West)

The walk begins by crossing meadows, partially encircles Cheddar reservoir, continues along enclosed tracks and finishes with a stroll beside two of the waterways of the Somerset Levels. It is a flat walk near the base of the steep Mendip escarpment and provides fine views both of the hills themselves and across the flat, watery expanses of the levels. Some parts are likely to be boggy and waterlogged after wet weather.

The square in the centre of Axbridge is a most attractive spot. Just beyond one corner of it stands the handsome and well-proportioned 15th-century cruciform church. In another corner is the picturesque King John's Hunting Lodge – in reality not a medieval lodge at all but the house of a Tudor merchant. It is now a museum.

Start in the village centre and walk along St Mary's Street, passing to the right of the church. After ⅓ mile (540m) turn right through a metal gate **Ⓐ**, at a public footpath sign, walk along an enclosed track and go through the left-hand of two gates in front. Continue along the right edge of a field towards the grassy reservoir embankment, climb a stile, turn left across grass and climb another stile to enter woodland.

At a fork take the left-hand track, cross a tarmac drive, climb a stile and continue across meadows. Both ahead

and to the left are attractive views of the wooded slopes of the Mendips. Go through a gate by a line of trees and keep ahead, by a wire fence bordering trees on the right. Over to the right are more fine views looking across the reservoir. Continue past a boatyard and, at a fork, do not bear right alongside the water but keep ahead across the meadow, parallel to the right-hand edge. Pass through a line of trees, keep along the right edge of woodland – likely to be marshy here – and continue through trees to a metal gate. Go through and keep ahead to a T-junction.

Turn left, go through a gate and turn right along a track **Ⓑ**. This is part of the Axbridge-Cheddar Cycleway which follows the route of the former Cheddar Valley Railway, nicknamed the 'Strawberry Line'. Over to the left, the gash that can be seen in the line of the Mendips is Cheddar Gorge. In front of a bridge turn right up steps, keep ahead to a lane and turn right along it **C**. In front of gates leading to a reservoir, bear left to continue along a pleasant, tree-lined track. When you reach the car park of the Cheddar Angling Club, bear left along an enclosed track.

Keep along this track to reach the Cheddar Yeo river. Cross a footbridge over it and turn right **D** alongside it. Go through a metal gate and at the next footbridge turn right **E** to re-cross the river. The final part of the walk is very attractive, with views ahead of Axbridge church tower and the Mendips in the background, as you keep along the right edge of a field by Ellenge

Grassy meadows on the route from Axbridge

Stream. Go through a metal gate, keep ahead, cross a footbridge and climb a stile. Continue, between a hedge on the left and the stream on the right, climb another stile and keep ahead along a track which continues as a lane into Axbridge. Turn right and at a T-junction, turn left to return to the village centre. ●

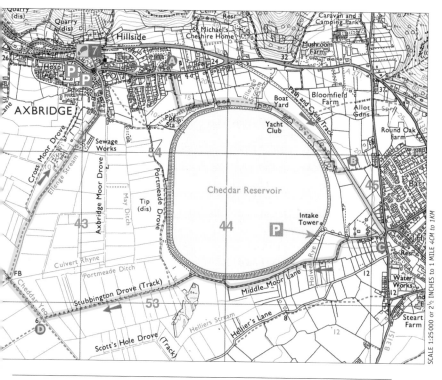

Salisbury and Old Sarum

Start	Salisbury
Distance	5½ miles (8.9km)
Approximate time	2½ hours
Parking	Salisbury
Refreshments	Pubs and cafés at Salisbury, light refreshments at Old Sarum, pub on main road near point **F**
Ordnance Survey maps	Landranger 184 (Salisbury & The Plain), Pathfinder 1241, SU03/13 (Salisbury (North))

There is considerable historic interest on this walk linking New Sarum (or Salisbury) in the Avon valley with Old Sarum, its predecessor, on the hill above. The first part of the route follows a delightful stretch of the River Avon to Stratford sub Castle before heading up to the remains of Old Sarum. From this hilltop position you enjoy extensive views over Salisbury, the Avon valley and Salisbury Plain before descending to rejoin the river. Allow plenty of time to explore both the beautiful cathedral city of Salisbury and the remains of Old Sarum.

The cathedral and city of Salisbury were built on a new site when the seat of the bishop was moved there from Old Sarum in 1220. As a result Salisbury is a rare example of a planned medieval city, laid out on a grid system. Around the spacious Market Place and Guildhall Square, the heart of the city, much of the original street pattern and a number of fine medieval buildings survive.

Standing in a green, walled close – the largest in England – and lined with an assortment of distinguished buildings from the Middle Ages to the 18th century, Salisbury is the only medieval cathedral conceived and completed as a whole. It was built in a remarkably short time, between 1220 and 1258, and therefore has a unique uniformity of design. Only the upper part of the tower and spire came later, in the early 14th century. The cathedral

is a supreme example of the Early English style, with an elaborate west front and lofty nave and choir. In such a spacious setting its beauty can be appreciated from all angles, but the undoubted crowning glory is the graceful, soaring spire, 404ft (123m) high, the tallest in the country.

The walk starts in the Market Place. Turn along the covered Market Walk, following signs to Riverside Walk, cross the River Avon and turn right on to a tarmac path beside it. This is part of the Wiltshire Cycleway and is signposted to Stratford and Old Sarum. Keep beside the river, passing to the right of car parks and going under several bridges and across roads, to reach a wooden bridge on the edge of parkland **A**.

From here continue along a gravel path beside the river, cross a bridge over a stream, pass to the right of a

children's play area and bear left to a metal barrier. Pass beside it and immediately turn right to continue along a gravel path across a field to a footpath sign where the path forks.

Take the right-hand path, rejoining the Avon, and continue along a lovely, tree-lined stretch of the river. Mud can be a problem on these low lying riverside meadows and part of the route is across boardwalks. Where these end, keep ahead, go through two metal gates and after the second one, continue across the meadow to a wire fence on the far side. Turn left here away from the river and follow the field edge as it curves first right, then left and finally right again to reach a metal kissing gate in the corner.

Go through, and a few yards ahead turn right along an enclosed path, which may be overgrown in the summer. Follow it to the left to a crossroads of paths **B**, turn right along a tarmac path, and cross a bridge over the Avon. Keep ahead, pass beside a metal barrier and continue to a T-junction in Stratford sub Castle. Ahead is a fine view of Old Sarum.

The ruins of the former glory of Old Sarum

Turn left along a road and just before it bears right by the church – medieval, but with a west tower that was rebuilt in 1711 – turn right on to an enclosed, tarmac path Ⓒ. The path heads uphill to a road Ⓓ; keep along it and after almost ½ mile (800m), turn right over a stile Ⓔ. Walk along a path beside the outer ramparts of Old Sarum on the right, heading gently uphill, climb a stile and a few yards ahead turn right on to a tarmac drive. Follow the drive around a right-hand bend Ⓕ to the entrance to Old Sarum.

Old Sarum is a fascinating place, for where else can you explore the site of an abandoned medieval city and, at the same time, look down on its successor? As early as the Iron Age a fort was established on this hilltop, but it was after the Norman Conquest that Old Sarum became a thriving city, with the headquarters of the diocese moving here in 1075, and the building of a castle. Several factors led to its decline – the combination of a cramped hilltop position, the lack of a water supply and quarrels between the cathedral and castle caused the bishop to move down the hill in 1220 and found New Sarum

or Salisbury. What remains today within the vast earthworks of the outer defences are the bishops' palace, the Norman cathedral and the foundations and some of the walls of the castle, which occupies the centre of the site. As an added bonus the views of the surrounding countryside are superb.

Retrace your steps to the bend in the drive Ⓕ, go through a gate and take a downhill path. Go through another gate, continue downhill and a few yards before reaching a road, turn right on to a track, at a public footpath sign to Stratford sub Castle. Continue by a hedge along the right edge of a field to a fork and take the left-hand enclosed path which heads downhill to the Parliament Stone, by a kissing gate on the right. Near here elections were held for the 'rotten borough' of Old Sarum, so called because, despite having only a handful of voters, it used to elect members to Parliament until such seats were abolished by the Great Reform Act of 1832.

Continue gently downhill and eventually the path broadens out into a track, which leads on to a road. Keep ahead and where the road bends right, turn left over a stile Ⓖ, at a public footpath sign to the City Centre, and walk along an enclosed path, between a hedge on the left and a wire fence bordering a meadow on the right. Later keep ahead along a pleasant, tree-lined tarmac track and where this ends, turn right and cross the wooden bridge over the River Avon Ⓐ, to rejoin the outward route.

Turn left beside the river and retrace your steps to the start. ●

Lacock and Bowden Park

Start	Lacock, NT car park on the edge of the village
Distance	6½ miles (10.5km)
Approximate time	3½ hours
Parking	National Trust car park at Lacock
Refreshments	Pubs and cafés at Lacock, pub just before point **E**
Ordnance Survey maps	Landranger 173 (Swindon & Devizes), Pathfinders 1168, ST87/97 (Chippenham & Castle Combe) and 1184, ST86/96 (Melksham)

This is a walk across fields and through woodland in the gentle countryside of the Avon valley to the north and east of the National Trust village of Lacock. There are some splendid views, especially on the descent through Bowden Park, and a pleasant finale across riverside meadows. Expect some overgrown and muddy paths in places and, as this is a fairly tortuous route, follow the directions carefully.

Cross the road from the car park and take the path through the trees, signposted 'Village, Abbey Museum and Shops'. At a road, turn left into Lacock. Renowned as one of England's most beautiful villages, Lacock is a harmonious mixture of stone and half-timbered buildings spanning the centuries from the 13th to the 19th. Like many of the nearby Cotswold villages, its wealth and prosperity were based on the medieval wool trade. One of its finest buildings is the mainly 14th- and 15th-century church, unusual in that although cruciform, it has a west tower and spire.

Lacock Abbey was originally an Augustinian monastery, founded in 1232, and when it was converted into a Tudor mansion after its closure in 1539, some of the medieval monastic buildings, including the cloisters and chapter house, were incorporated into the new structure. Further alterations

were made in the 18th and 19th centuries. In the middle years of the 19th century it was the home of William Henry Fox Talbot, pioneer of modern photography, and there is a museum commemorating his work near the abbey entrance. Both abbey and village were given to the National Trust in 1944.

Turn right opposite the Red Lion, at a T-junction turn right again and in front of the church turn left along a lane, at a No Through Road sign. Cross a footbridge over a brook, by a ford, then at a fork take the right-hand tarmac path to rejoin the lane. Walk uphill to where the lane ends in front of a fence.

Ahead are three paths: take the one to the right, passing through a kissing gate, and follow a tarmac path across a field to another kissing gate on the far side. Go through, continue along an enclosed path to a road, keep ahead for a few yards and turn right to cross the

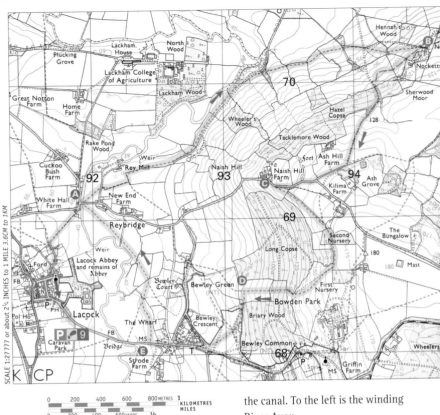

SCALE 1:27777 or about 2¾ INCHES to 1 MILE 3.6CM to 1KM

0	200	400	600	800 METRES	1
					KILOMETRES
					MILES
0	200	400	600 YARDS	½

bridge over the River Avon Ⓐ. Turn left over a metal stile, at a public footpath sign, and walk diagonally across a field, making for another metal stile. Climb it, cross a tarmac drive, climb a metal stile opposite and keep along a narrow, enclosed path. The path curves right, then bends left and you climb two more metal stiles in quick succession before emerging into a field.

Turn left along the field edge, follow it to the right, go through a gap in the hedge on the left and then turn right to keep along the top edge of the next field, now with the hedge on the right. At the far end follow the narrow path ahead through an area of scrub and trees along the left side of a disused canal – it might be overgrown here – then continue through trees to a stile. Climb it and keep ahead across a field, alongside the mostly dried-up bed of

the canal. To the left is the winding River Avon.

Go through a gate into another area of scrub and trees, bear right to a stile, climb it and turn left along the left edge of a field, by a wire fence bordering trees on the left. Climb a stile in the field corner, keep ahead in the same direction across the next field, climb another stile and continue through more scrub and trees. Head up to climb a stile, keep ahead across a field, later continuing by a hedge on the left, and go through a metal gate just to the right of a hedge corner. Continue along the left edge of the next field, cross a track, then bear slightly right away from the field edge and head diagonally uphill to a stile in the far corner.

Climb it and continue in the same direction across the next field, bearing right on joining a track on the far side. A few yards in front of a metal gate – and by another metal gate on the left – turn sharp right Ⓑ and head back along the top edge of the field just crossed, passing through a hedge gap just to the right of the field corner. Walk across the next field, climb a stile and keep in the same direction across the next field, bearing left to join a tarmac track on the edge of woodland. Go through a metal gate, head gently uphill through the wood, bear right and go through a gate to the right of a cattlegrid, here emerging from the trees.

Continue along the track, at first along the right edge of a field and then heading gently uphill across fields and curving right to a metal gate. Go through, continue along the track – now enclosed – to a narrow lane and turn right along it. Where the lane curves slightly right just before a farm, turn left over a stile ⒞. From here there is a grand view over the Avon valley.

After climbing the stile turn sharp left to keep along the left edge of a field, then bear slightly away from it to climb a stile and continue by a wire fence along the left edge of the next field. Climb a stile in the corner to enter woodland, continue through it and at a T-junction of paths, turn right to a stile. Climb it, keep by woodland and a hedge along the right edge of a field, and just before reaching the field corner, turn right over a waymarked stile.

Head diagonally downhill across Bowden Park – there is a superb view ahead over the Avon valley with the 18th-century house to the left. Bear gradually right towards the bottom corner of the woodland on the right, and aim for the gap between two belts of woodland. In the bottom right-hand corner of the field, turn right along a track to a stile, climb it, continue downhill across a field and climb another

stile beside a gate. Keep ahead and when you are parallel with the corner of the wood on the left, turn left ⒟ and head across the field towards a house. Climb a stile, continue along an enclosed track and where it bears left towards a gatehouse, bear right and head diagonally across the open expanse of Bewley Common to a road.

Turn right along it, heading gently downhill all the while, and about 200 yds (183m) before reaching the bridge over the river, turn right over a stile ⒠, at a public footpath sign, and head across the riverside meadows. To the left is a fine view of Lacock Abbey across the Avon. Bear right towards the hedge on the right edge of the meadow and look out for a footbridge over a ditch and a waymarked stile. Climb the stile, keep by a hedge along the left edge of a field, climb another stile and bear slightly right across the next field, making for a hedge gap, metal gate and public footpath sign. Climb a stile to the left of the gate and keep ahead by the banks of the placid Avon.

Climb a stile, keep ahead across the meadow – cutting a corner where the river does a loop to the left – and continue to a stile to the right of the bridge. Climb it on to a road, turn left over the bridge ⒜ and retrace your steps from here into Lacock. ●

The picturesque village of Lacock

Fovant Down

Start	Fovant, by the church at the north end of the village
Distance	4½ miles (7.2km)
Approximate time	2 hours
Parking	By Fovant church
Refreshments	Pubs at Fovant
Ordnance Survey maps	Landranger 184 (Salisbury & The Plain), Pathfinders 1261, ST82/92 (Shaftesbury) and 1262, SU02/12 (Salisbury (South) & Broad Chalke)

There are poignant memories of World War I both at the start of the walk in Fovant churchyard and on Fovant Down, famed for its carvings of regimental badges. After an initial ascent and descent to the west of the village, a steady climb leads on to the crest of the down followed by a walk along the wooded ridge. The views from here are superb. The descent takes you across the face of the down past some of the badges, though these are best viewed from the bottom. The final part of the walk is through the attractive village of Fovant.

At the start of the walk you might like to enter the peaceful and attractive churchyard of Fovant's medieval church. Here are the graves of soldiers from all over the British Empire who died from injuries received during World War I.

Begin by walking back along the lane to a crossroads, turn left and at a public bridleway sign to the A30, turn right on to a tarmac track **Ⓐ**. After a few yards this becomes a grassy path, enclosed between hedges and trees, which heads gently uphill through a steep-sided valley to a fork.

Continue along the right-hand enclosed path – this is narrow and likely to be overgrown – which descends gently to reach the A30 to the right of a farm **Ⓑ**. Cross over and take the lane ahead, signposted to Broad Chalke and Bowerchalke. Where the lane bends right in front of a chalk pit, bear left over a stile **Ⓒ**, at a public footpath sign to Fovant Down. Continue along the sunken path ahead, climbing steadily up to the ridge of the down, head up through bushes near the top and turn

The church at Fovant

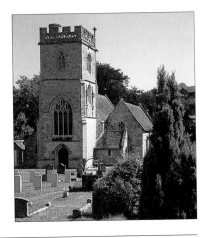

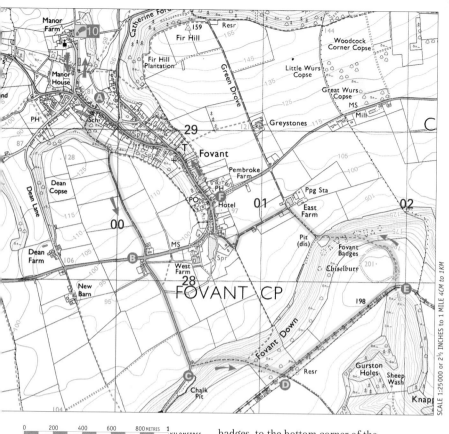

SCALE 1:25000 or 2½ INCHES to 1 MILE 4CM to 1KM

```
0        200      400      600      800 METRES  1
                                            KILOMETRES
                                            MILES
0        200      400      600 YARDS    ½
```

right over a stile to a crossroads **D**. Turn left and walk along a broad, ridge top track through a narrow strip of woodland. After emerging into open country, extensive views open up across the sweeping downs on both sides.

Where the track curves right, turn left over a stile **E** and keep ahead along the right edge of the earthworks of Chiselbury Fort, an Iron Age hill fort which, at a height of 662ft (201m), enjoys a commanding position and magnificent views. Shortly after following the curve of the fort gradually to the left, look out for a stile in a fence on the right and head across to climb it.

Bear left and follow a faint, grassy path steeply and diagonally downhill, passing between some of the regimental badges, to the bottom corner of the down. Continue through bushes, keep ahead to climb a stile and walk along the left edge of a field to a metal gate in the corner. At this point look back for a good view of the Fovant Badges, a series of regimental badges carved on the side of the down by troops stationed here in World War I.

Go through the gate and turn left along a straight, enclosed track, passing to the left of a large farmhouse. Later the track bears left, then turns right and continues between houses to emerge on to a lane on the edge of Fovant. Keep ahead through the village to the main road, cross over and continue along the lane opposite through this long and strung out village. At a fork in front of the villge hall take the left-hand lane, signposted to Tisbury, and at a crossroads turn right along Church Lane to return to the start. ●

Old and New Wardour Castles

Start	Old Wardour Castle, signposted from the A30 to the east of Shaftesbury
Distance	4 miles (6.4km)
Approximate time	2 hours
Parking	Old Wardour Castle
Refreshments	Refreshment kiosk at Old Wardour Castle
Ordnance Survey maps	Landranger 184 (Salisbury & The Plain), Pathfinder 1261, ST82/92 (Shaftesbury)

A ruined medieval castle and its 18th-century successor are linked by this undulating and interesting walk near the northern edge of Cranborne Chase. The route passes through a varied and attractive mixture of landscaped parkland, farmland and woodland. There is some modest climbing on the latter stages and a final descent through woodland.

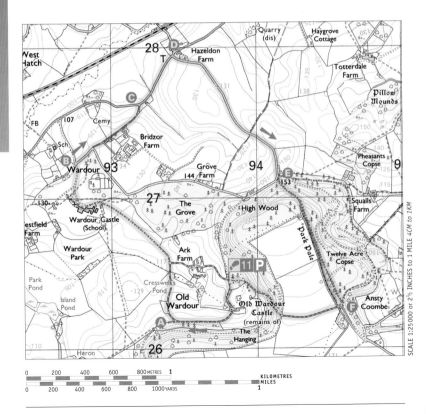

SCALE 1:25000 or 2½ INCHES to 1 MILE 4CM to 1KM

The ruins of Old Wardour Castle are much enhanced by their romantic setting in landscaped grounds beside a lake. The hexagonal-shaped castle dates from the 14th century, but after its purchase by the Arundell family in 1570 it was partially rebuilt and made more comfortable. After the Civil War it was abandoned and fell into ruin but the landscaping of the grounds in the 18th century led to the building of a 'Gothick' summer house and the construction of a grotto, a popular contemporary feature.

Start by taking the tarmac track that leads from the car park, passing between the castle on the left and the lake on the right. After passing to the right of the castle's 18th-century summer house, the track bends to the right and continues as a rough track. Later it becomes enclosed and keeps along the right inside edge of sloping woodland. To the right are grand views across the parkland.

By a waymarked post on the left, turn right ⓐ on to a clear track that curves left and heads gently downhill between wire fences. Keep ahead through a metal gate, following Wessex Ridgeway signs, go through another one and continue towards the imposing bulk of the new Wardour Castle, a grand

The medieval ruins of Old Wardour Castle

Georgian mansion built for the Arundells between 1770 and 1776. The house was sold after World War II and later used as a girls' school.

Bear right to pass in front of the house, curve right again and pass between stone gateposts on to a lane ⓑ. Turn right and where the lane bends right, continue along the tarmac track to Bridzor Farm. Pass to the left of the farm, go through a metal gate and keep ahead, descending to a road ⓒ. Turn right, head uphill and at the top – just before a telephone box – turn right along a lane ⓓ.

Walk gently uphill along this tree-lined lane and keep along it for ¾ mile (1.2km) to where it bears right. At this point keep ahead ⓔ along the track to Fox Farm, entering woodland. The track climbs quite steeply through the trees – at the top pass to the left of the farm and continue through an area of mixed woodland, a most attractive part of the walk. At a junction of paths and tracks, turn right ⓕ along a track to emerge from the trees, and at a crossroads keep ahead along an enclosed track across fields. The track then re-enters woodland and descends, passing under an arch, to the start. ●

Weston Woods and Sand Bay

Start	Sand Bay car park, ½ mile (800m) west of Kewstoke village
Distance	6 miles (9.7km)
Approximate time	3 hours
Parking	Sand Bay
Refreshments	Hotel and café near start, pub at Kewstoke, pub at Sand Bay at point Ⓖ
Ordnance Survey maps	Landranger 182 (Weston-super-Mare & Bridgwater), Pathfinder 1181, ST26/36 (Weston-super-Mare)

To the north of the popular resort of Weston-super-Mare the lovely Weston Woods clothe the slopes of Worlebury Hill and give fine views along the length of Sand Bay and across the Bristol Channel to the coast of South Wales. A large proportion of this walk is through these woods, with a brief foray into Weston (as Weston-super-Mare is known locally). The latter part of the route takes you down the medieval Monk's Steps and across fields, with a final section along the shores of Sand Bay.

From the car park turn right along the road, head uphill to a T-junction and turn right, signposted Weston-super-Mare Toll Road. In front of the Castle Restaurant bear left Ⓐ, at a sign to Weston Woods, on to a track that climbs steadily through the trees. Keep ahead all the while on the main track to reach a crossroads of tracks at the top.

Turn right, passing to the right of a reservoir and radio masts, and continue in a straight line through the woods and eventually the track gently descends to reach a road by Weston's Old Pier Ⓑ. Walk along the road, at a fork take the left-hand

road, passing above the pier and gardens, and at the next fork take the left-hand road again (South Road) which curves left. Opposite a church

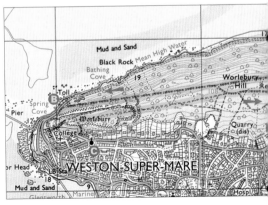

turn left ⓒ into Trinity Road and head uphill, then turn sharp right and where the road ends, take the path ahead to re-enter Weston Woods

Turn left, climb a flight of steps and at the top turn right along a path that passes through the remains of Worlebury Hillfort, an Iron Age defence. Continue straight ahead along the path as it broadens out into a track, ignoring all side paths and keeping roughly parallel to the outward route. After passing to the right of the reservoir and masts, the track becomes even wider and eventually emerges from the woods to continue as a road through a suburban housing area.

At a crossroads in front of Worlebury golf club, turn left ⓓ along Monks Hill, turn left again into Woodspring Avenue and after 50 yds (46m) – by a bench and bus stop – turn right ⓔ to descend the Monk's Steps, constructed by the monks of nearby Woodspring Priory in the Middle Ages. It is quite a long descent, between trees and with fine views ahead over Sand Bay, but take care as the steps are uneven and might be slippery. At the bottom cross a road, turn left and then almost immediately turn right over a stone stile, at a public footpath sign, and descend some more difficult steps. Continue along a path, by a fence on the right, descend a few more steps and go through a squeezer stile on to a road opposite Kewstoke's fine medieval church.

Turn right, take the first turning on the left (Crooks Lane) and where the road curves left, bear right ⓕ, at a public footpath sign, along a tarmac path. After passing to the right of a house, it continues as a narrow, enclosed path. Go through a metal kissing gate and continue along the right edge of several low-lying fields, which could be boggy and waterlogged at times, keeping by a hedge on the right and crossing a series of footbridges over ditches. Finally keep along an enclosed, hedge-lined path to a metal kissing gate, go through and continue along a tarmac drive in front of a holiday camp. Where the drive turns left, keep ahead across a grassy area, making for a gap in the far left-hand corner.

Turn left along a tarmac drive beside the Long John Silver pub to a road and turn left ⓖ along the promenade beside Sand Bay to return to the start. On this last leg there are fine views ahead of the wooded headland of Worlebury Hill and to the right across the expanses of the bay to the coast of South Wales. ●

Avebury, West Kennett and Silbury Hill

Start	Avebury
Distance	6½ miles (10.5km)
Approximate time	3 hours
Parking	National Trust car park at Avebury
Refreshments	Pub and café at Avebury
Ordnance Survey maps	Landranger 173 (Swindon & Devizes), Pathfinders 1169, SU07/17 (Marlborough Downs) and 1185, SU06/16 (Devizes & Marlborough)

This fascinating walk links the most outstanding collection of prehistoric remains in the country. From the stone circle at Avebury, the route heads up on to the downs and follows a section of the Ridgeway into the village of East Kennett. It then continues to the impressive West Kennett Long Barrow, and the final stretch, mainly by the infant River Kennet, takes you past the intriguing Silbury Hill, the largest artificial mound in Europe. Allow plenty of time in order to appreciate these unique monuments to the full.

A 17th-century antiquarian wrote of the great stone circle at Avebury that 'it did as much excel Stonehenge, as a cathedral does a parish church'. Constructed sometime between 2700 and 1700 BC and the focal point of the most important group of prehistoric monuments in the country, it is undeniably impressive, even in an incomplete state. It is also more complex than it seems, with two smaller circles within the main outer ring of stones, and protected by a ditch and embankment. The size of the circle and the proximity of the other monuments suggest that it must have been a major political and/or religious centre of Neolithic Britain.

Partially enclosed by the stone circle, the village of Avebury is a most attractive place in its own right, with an Elizabethan manor house and fine medieval church. Begin by taking the tarmac path, signposted Avebury Village and Stone Circle, that leads from the far corner of the car park. Follow it to a road and turn right **Ⓐ** through the village, passing through the outer circle. Where the road turns left by the Red Lion, keep straight ahead along a lane (Green Street). Pass through the stone circle again and after passing a farm, the lane becomes a rough track which heads steadily uphill on to a ridge.

At a crossroads of tracks turn right on to the Ridgeway **Ⓑ** and follow a track across the downs. The views from here are extensive and wide ranging. Eventually the track descends gently to

SCALE 1:26316 or about 2½ INCHES to 1 MILE 3.8CM to 1KM

```
0    200   400   600   800 METRES  1
                                      KILOMETRES
                                      MILES
0    200   400   600 YARDS  ½
```

emerge on to the busy A4 **C**. To the left is a group of tumuli and on the other side of the road is the Sanctuary, formerly a double circle of stones linked to Avebury by a stone avenue. Some of the stones that formed this processional avenue survive beside the lane between West Kennett and Avebury.

Walk along the enclosed track opposite, continue downhill along the right edge of a field and in the bottom corner follow the field edge round to the left to a footpath sign. Turn right through a gap, cross a bridge over the River Kennet and continue along a tarmac drive to a lane. Keep ahead but after a few yards turn right **D** at a wall corner along an enclosed path, which leads to a lane. Here turn right through the village of East Kennett and just before the lane crosses the river, turn left along a track.

At a junction of tracks and paths, keep straight ahead along a tree-lined track for a few yards , then turn right

E on to a path enclosed by trees, with a wire fence on the right. Climb a stile and walk along the left edge of a field, following the field edge as it bears to the left. Climb a stile at the far end, cross a tarmac track and continue along the track ahead. Where it ends, keep along the right edge of a field and, in the field corner, go through a gap on to a well-surfaced path **F**.

The route continues ahead but turn left and head gently uphill in order to visit West Kennett Long Barrow. This stone-chambered tomb, dating from around 3700 BC, is the largest burial chamber in England, nearly 350ft (107m) long. The three huge stones at the entrance were probably placed there when the tomb was sealed up.

As you retrace your steps downhill, the view is dominated by the imposing bulk of Silbury Hill. Follow the path to the left, turn right through a metal kissing gate and cross a bridge over the river. Keep ahead and go through

another metal kissing gate on to the A4. Turn left and soon after crossing the River Kennet again you arrive at Silbury Hill, the largest man-made mound in Europe, 130ft (40m) high and covering an area of over 5 acres. So well built was it that there has hardly been any erosion over a period of nearly 5000 years. However, investigations and excavations have failed to find out the exact purpose of this incredible feat of construction, which remains one of the great mysteries of prehistory.

Walk back along the road and just after re-crossing the river, turn left over a stile to continue along the left edge of a field, by a wire fence and later the river on the left. Follow the Kennet back to Avebury, negotiating a number of stiles and gates. On reaching a road, turn right and almost immediately left into the car park. ●

The stones of West Kennett Long Barrow

Glastonbury

Start	Glastonbury
Distance	6½ miles (10.5km)
Approximate time	3½ hours
Parking	Glastonbury
Refreshments	Pubs and cafés at Glastonbury
Ordnance Survey maps	Landranger 182 (Weston-super-Mare & Bridgwater), Explorer 4 (Mendip Hills West)

Shrouded in mystery and steeped in early Christian and Arthurian legends, the Isle of Avalon around Glastonbury is one of a number of 'islands' that rise above the surrounding marshy and formerly waterlogged 'moors' of the Somerset Levels. This route passes all the well-known sites associated with these legends, beginning with a walk across part of the levels and along the banks of the River Brue, and continuing over Wearyall and Chalice Hills. Highlight of the walk is the steep climb to the top of the distinctive, conical-shaped Glastonbury Tor, in sight for most of the way and a superb vantage point.

According to legend, St Joseph of Arimathea visited Britain around AD 60 and came to Glastonbury. While here he is said to have founded the first Christian church; stuck his staff in the ground on Wearyall Hill, causing it to grow and flower into the Glastonbury Thorn; and hidden the Holy Grail, the cup used by Christ at the Last Supper, beneath a well on Chalice Hill. Later legends linked Glastonbury with the semi-mythical King Arthur, and both he and his wife Guinevere are said to be buried in the abbey, the site of their alleged tomb now marked by a plaque.

If some of the legends are true, Glastonbury may well be the oldest Christian site in Britain. It is possible that a church was established here in the late Roman period, but the first concrete evidence is the founding of a monastery in the early 7th century.

During the Middle Ages this was to become the wealthiest and most powerful in the country, its wealth largely based on its legendary associations. The existing ruins of Glastonbury Abbey are mainly of the church that was rebuilt after a great fire in 1184 and enough survives to give some idea of its size and splendour.

In the town there is further evidence of the power and influence wielded by the medieval abbots. The 15th-century George and Pilgrims Inn probably originated as a guest house for the thousands of pilgrims who came here. The abbot held court in the 15th-century Abbot's Tribunal, now the Tourist Information Centre, and the 14th-century Abbey Barn, now a museum of rural life, used to store the produce brought to the abbey by its many tenants.

Start at the Market Cross in the town centre and turn down Benedict Street. Shortly after passing Fairfield Gardens on the left, turn right **A** on to a tarmac track and, after it narrows to a path, turn left across a grassy area to climb a stile. Cross a road and take the road opposite, but almost immediately turn right over a stile. Keep along the left edge of a field and climb another stile on to the busy bypass.

Cross over, look out for a stile at the side of a factory, climb it, pass in front of factory buildings and turn right along a lane. The lane bends left to cross a drainage channel and then bends right to continue alongside it. At a public footpath sign to Aqueduct Crossing, turn left through a gate **B**, and keep along the right bank of a channel (formerly the course of a canal) for the next ¾ mile (1.2km), crossing a footbridge and a lane and eventually climbing up an embankment above the River Brue. Turn left through a gate, turn right to cross a bridge over the river and turn left along a road **C**.

Turn left over the first bridge, turn right through a gate **D** and keep beside the left bank of the Brue, passing through several gates as the river curves left to reach a bridge – the Pons Perilis, or Pomparles Bridge **E**. Climb a stile on to a road, turn left and immediately turn right into Roman Way.

After the road curves left and then bends right, look out for some steps on the left. Go up them, pass by a stone barrier and bear right to climb steadily over Wearyall Hill. The view from the top extends across the Somerset Levels to the lines of the Mendips and Quantocks on the horizon; nearer at hand is the Tor, with the town and abbey ruins nestling below it. The alleged thorn which grew here was destroyed by a zealous Puritan in the 17th century but cuttings from it still

survive at various sites, including one in the abbey grounds.

Descend to a stile, climb it on to a lane **F** and follow it downhill to a crossroads. Turn right downhill along Butleigh Road and at the bottom turn left into Bretnoux Road **G**. Climb a stile on the right and turn left to walk along the left edge of a field, keeping parallel to the road. Follow the field edge to the left and right and continue along it, by a hedge on the left. In the field corner turn left over a stile on to a lane **H**, turn left to a T-junction, then turn left again and at a public footpath sign 'To the Tor', turn right over a stile. Head diagonally across a field, climb a stile, turn right to climb another and bear left. Pass through a gap, head up to climb another stile and continue uphill across a field, making for a stile in the far left corner in front of a house. Climb it, walk along an enclosed path and go through a gate on to a road.

Turn left and take the first turning on the right (Well House Lane) **J**. Ahead is

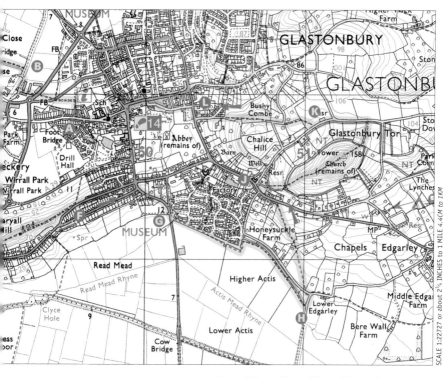

SCALE 1:22727 or about 2¾ INCHES to 1 MILE 4.4CM to 1KM

the Chalice Well, where the water is stained red allegedly because this is where Joseph of Arimathea left the Holy Grail containing the blood of Christ – mineral deposits in the soil may offer a more down to earth explanation. Almost immediately after turning into Well House Lane, the route turns right again, at a 'To the Tor' footpath stone, along an enclosed, uphill path which curves left to a squeezer stile. Go through and follow the uphill path ahead – paved in places, with steps and several zigzags – to the tower on the top of Glastonbury Tor. Despite a modest height of only 520ft (158m) the climb is quite steep, but the reward is a magnificent view over the surrounding flat country to the Bristol Channel, the Mendips, Quantocks and, in clear conditions, Exmoor and South Wales. The 15th-century tower is all that remains of St Michael's Chapel, where medieval pilgrims used to pray before the last leg of the journey to Glastonbury. In 1539 the last abbot was

hanged here for resisting Henry VIII's dissolution of the monasteries.

At the tower turn right, descend steps and follow a concrete path downhill. Go through a kissing gate at the bottom on to a lane. Turn left, continue downhill and at a public footpath sign turn right over a stile **Ⓚ**. Cross a field, climb a stile and continue along an enclosed path to another one. Climb that, turn right along a track to a lane, keep ahead and where the lane bends sharply left, continue along a path. Go through a metal kissing gate, keep ahead along the top edge of a meadow and descend Chalice Hill to reach a metal squeezer stile. Go through, keep ahead to a road and walk along it to a T-junction. Turn right and take the first turning on the left (Silver Street) **Ⓛ**. Where the street ends, turn right along a lane into High Street opposite St John's church and turn left to return to the start. ●

Lambourn Downs

Start	Lambourn
Distance	7 miles (11.3km)
Approximate time	3 hours
Parking	Lambourn
Refreshments	Pubs and café at Lambourn
Ordnance Survey maps	Landranger 174 (Newbury & Wantage), Pathfinders 1154, SU28/38 (Lambourn Downs) and 1170, SU27/37 (Lambourn & Aldbourne)

There could hardly be a more typical downland walk than this with wide and clear tracks, gentle gradients and expansive views across open, rolling country. Be prepared to share the walk with riders exercising their horses as the Lambourn Downs are very much horse racing country.

Much of the business and prosperity of the pleasant village of Lambourn revolves around horse racing. The walk starts in the Market Place by the medieval church, an unusually grand building with a fine Norman nave and west front.

Take the paved path to the right of the church, marked by a Lambourn Valley Way footpath sign. The path passes to the left of the brick gatehouse to some picturesque 19th-century almshouses, and emerges via a gate on to a road. Keep ahead along this tree-lined road for ½ mile (800m) and where

The open landscape of Lambourn Downs

it curves slightly left, continue along the path on the right Ⓐ which bears right at a public footpath sign and heads across a field.

On reaching a lane by the Malt Shovel, turn left through Upper Lambourn, passing some thatched cottages. Where the lane ends, keep ahead along a tarmac path called Fulke Walwyn Way – there is a parallel horse track to the right – and where path and track unite, turn right Ⓑ along a sunken, narrow, tree-lined tarmac track which heads steadily uphill.

Where this track bends sharply right, keep ahead, following Byway and Lambourn Valley Way signs, over a crossroads of tracks and at a fork take the left-hand, hedge-lined track on to the downs Ⓒ. At a junction of tracks keep ahead, passing to the right of a Dutch barn, and now come fine, open views across the sweeping, rolling downs as you continue along a gently undulating track.

At a Byway sign – about 100 yds (91m) before the track curves left – turn

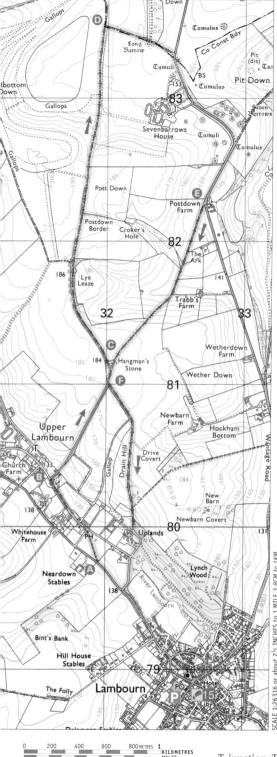

right **D** on to a grassy track. Keep ahead along the left-hand track at a fork, skirt the right edge of woodland, pass between wooden barriers and continue to a lane. Turn right, follow the lane ahead and round a right-hand bend. At this point a brief detour along the track to the left leads to Seven Barrows, a nature reserve comprising ungrazed chalk grassland in the midst of which are seven Bronze Age barrows, dating from between 1800 and 500 BC.

Continue along the lane and where it curves left by Postdown Farm, bear right **E** on to a track that heads steadily uphill over the downs again. The track later narrows to a hedge-lined path to reach a Byway sign where a track joins from the right. Keep ahead, briefly rejoining the outward route, over a crossroads of tracks and at a fork a few yards ahead, take the left-hand tarmac track **F**.

At the next fork continue along the right-hand track which heads gently downhill, later keeps along the right inside edge of woodland and becomes a tarmac lane. The lane turns left, then curves right and continues down to a T-junction. Turn left and retrace your steps to the start.

SCALE 1:26 316 or about 2½ INCHES to 1 MILE 3.8CM to 1KM

Uffington Monuments and Vale of the White Horse

Start	National Trust's Uffington White Horse and Wayland's Smithy car park, on Whitehorse Hill to the south of the B4507
Distance	6½ miles (10.5km)
Approximate time	3 hours
Parking	National Trust car park
Refreshments	Pub at Woolstone
Ordnance Survey maps	Landranger 174 (Newbury & Wantage), Pathfinder 1154, SU28/38 (Lambourn Downs)

On the slope of the downs, overlooking the Vale of the White Horse and just over the Oxfordshire border, is a group of prehistoric remains that is only eclipsed by the Avebury and Stonehenge complexes. The Uffington Monuments comprise Uffington Castle and the famous White Horse, plus Wayland's Smithy which is about 1½ miles (2.4km) away. From the crest of the downs the route descends into the vale to the village of Woolstone, then climbs back up, and the last part follows a superb stretch of the Ridgeway. As well as the considerable historic interest, the views, both over the downs to the south and the Vale of the White Horse to the north, are magnificent.

In the car park go up steps to a National Trust sign 'White Horse Hill', go through a gate, bear right and follow a worn grassy path across the down. Ahead the outline of the White Horse of Uffington can be seen. Noted for its futuristic design, this is the oldest and best known of all the white horses in England, but the nature of the connection between it and the nearby fort is uncertain.

Cross a lane and keep ahead, at a public bridleway sign, up the slopes of White Horse Hill, skirting the earthworks of Uffington Castle on the right. This Iron Age hillfort, which dates from around 500 BC, stands 856ft

(261m) above the Vale of the White Horse and is a superb viewpoint.

Bear right to the triangulation pillar, continue past it to a gate and go through on to the Ridgeway **Ⓐ**. Turn left and, at a fence corner, turn left over a stile **Ⓑ**, at a public footpath sign, and walk along by a wire fence on the right-hand edge of a field. As you gently descend, more superb views unfold over the vale. Where the fence turns right, bear right and head across to rejoin it, cutting a corner. The path curves left, passing to the right of the White Horse, and continues down to a lane. Cross it and bear right on to the footpath opposite which passes to the left of the

distinctive, flat-topped Dragon Hill.
This natural chalk outcrop, artificially
levelled on top, is by tradition the place
where St George slew the dragon.

Bear left, continue gently downhill,
passing to the right of a circular pit, and
climb a stile in the fence in front.
Continue downhill across the next field
and climb a stile on to the B4507 **C**.
Turn left along this winding road for
nearly ¹/₂ mile (800m), – it is from here
that you get some of the best views of
the White Horse.

Opposite a turning on the left, turn
right along a lane **D**, signposted to

Woolstone, and head quite steeply
downhill. Turn right over a stile and go
through a gate, at a public footpath
sign, head across a field, negotiate
another gate/stile combination and keep
ahead to the left of Woolstone's small
medieval church. Turn left along a
tarmac drive and follow it into the
village, rejoining the lane.

At a T-junction by the thatched
White Horse pub, turn left **E** and where
the lane bends right, keep ahead, at a
public footpath sign, along a track to a
stile. Climb it, bear slightly right to walk
along the left edge of a field, go
through a gate, continue along the edge
of the next field and climb a stile to
reach a T-junction of paths. Turn left

along an enclosed, tree- and hedge-lined path – Hardwell Lane – which ascends gently to emerge on to the B4507 again **F**.

Turn right and while passing the edge of Hardwell Wood, look out for a public footpath sign in the trees and turn left here **G** along a path to a stile. Climb it, follow a pleasant sunken path steadily uphill through the wood, climb another stile and continue up to emerge into a field. Head straight across it to a fingerpost on the far side where you rejoin the Ridgeway **H**.

Turn right along it to Wayland's Smithy, reached by turning right **J** through a kissing gate, at a footpath sign, and walking along a track. This burial chamber, which lies in a beautiful, secluded spot amongst trees, was named by the Saxons who thought that it must have been built by one of their gods, Wayland the Smith. In fact it is a Neolithic tomb, built around 3500 BC, with a new one constructed on top of it about 200 years later.

Return to the Ridgeway and turn left along it, climbing gently on to White Horse Hill and enjoying the grand views ahead and on both sides. On reaching the earthworks of Uffington Castle at the top, turn left through a gate **A**, at a public bridleway sign, and retrace your steps to the start.

The Vale of the White Horse

Ham Hill, Montacute and Norton Sub Hamdon

Start	Ham Hill Country Park
Distance	6 miles (9.7km)
Approximate time	3 hours
Parking	Ham Hill Country Park, near the Prince of Wales pub
Refreshments	Pub at the country park, pubs and cafés at Montacute, pubs at Norton Sub Hamdon
Ordnance Survey maps	Landranger 193 (Taunton & Lyme Regis), Pathfinder 1279, ST41/51 (Yeovil & Merriott)

Ham Hill Country Park occupies a ridge that rises to over 300ft (91m) and commands superb views over the surrounding countryside. There is an Iron Age hillfort on the site and over the years the land has been extensively quarried. From the starting point you descend through woodland to the village of Montacute, with two brief optional detours. The first of these is a climb to the magnificent viewpoint of St Michael's Hill, and the second is a visit to the 16th-century Montacute House. From Montacute an undulating route leads to the village of Norton Sub Hamdon, and finally comes a fairly steep climb to regain the ridge.

Start in front of the Prince of Wales pub and, at public footpath signs to East Stoke and Montacute, take the path that leads into woodland. At a fence corner a few yards ahead, turn left to descend steps and at the bottom turn right and continue through the trees.

Ignore a footpath sign to East Stoke on the left and keep near the left inside edge of Hedgecock Hill Wood to a T-junction of paths and tracks. Turn left downhill along a track, turn right and continue through this beautiful woodland, keeping on the main track and close to the left edge of the trees all the while. Eventually the track bears left downhill to a metal gate. Go through, bear right along an enclosed track and where the track turns left, turn right up

steps to a gate. Go through and continue along a grassy path as far as the first tree **Ⓐ**. At this point turn left for the detour to St Michael's Hill. Head across the grass to a National Trust sign, climb a stile here and bear left to follow a path steeply uphill through trees to the top, crowned by a tower, an 18th-century folly. The magnificent view encompasses Ham Hill, the Somerset Levels, Quantocks, Mendips and Dorset Downs.

Retrace your steps to point **Ⓐ** and turn left to rejoin the main route. Continue along a grassy path, later keeping by a wire fence on the left, curve left to follow the base of St Michael's Hill and descend gently along the right edge of woodland. At a

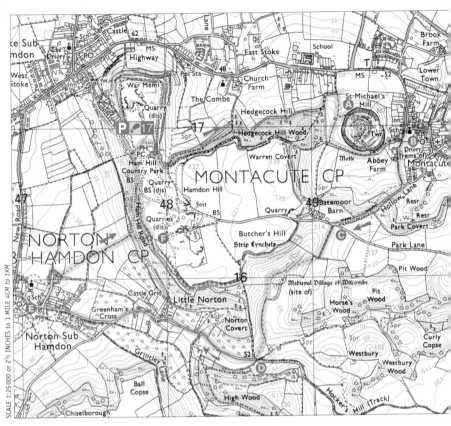

fork and 'Permissive Path Circular Walk' sign, take the right-hand path and continue gently downhill between tree-lined embankments to a gate. Go through, keep ahead along a tarmac drive, passing the gatehouse of a former Cluniac priory on the right, and go through another gate to a T-junction, where there is a public bridleway sign to Hollow Lane Ⓑ.

The route continues to the right, but for a brief and very worthwhile detour, turn left and first right into the idyllic village of Montacute, with its cottages built of the warm brown and honey-coloured hamstone quarried locally, and an attractive medieval church that retains a Norman chancel arch. From The Borough, the handsome square in the village centre, a road leads off to Montacute House, an imposing Elizabethan mansion built between 1588 and 1601. Among its many attractions are a collection of 17th- and 18th-century furniture, Elizabethan and Jacobean portraits and a formal garden and landscaped park. It is now owned by the National Trust.

Retrace your steps to the bridleway sign to Hollow Lane and keep ahead along a stony track, passing to the right of a duck pond. On reaching a gate, go through and keep ahead along an ascending track, then go through another gate at the top and turn right to continue uphill along a lane. At a public footpath sign to Park Lane on the left, go up steps and head uphill along a sunken, enclosed path through woodland to a stile. Climb it, bear right along the right edge of a field and in the corner climb a stile on to a lane to the left of a junction Ⓒ.

Turn right and at a public footpath sign to Witcombe, turn left along an enclosed track. At a T-junction turn right over a stile – bumps in the field ahead are all that remain of the deserted village of Witcombe – then turn left and head downhill into the bottom of the valley. Climb another stile, follow the path to a fence corner and continue along the bottom edge of a field, by a wire fence on the left, towards woodland in front. Eventually the path curves right to a stile beside a metal gate. Climb it and keep ahead to a tarmac track **D**.

Turn right and follow this pleasant, narrow track through the hamlet of Little Norton. Later keep ahead along a lane, continue along the right-hand lane at a fork and walk through the picturesque, thatched village of Norton Sub Hamdon. The church, built in the late 15th and early 16th centuries, is dominated by its grand 98ft (29m) high Perpendicular tower.

Turn right beside the Lord Nelson **E** along Rectory Lane and where the tarmac lane ends, keep ahead along a tarmac track to reach a kissing gate and public footpath sign on the right. Ahead is the ridge of Ham Hill and its war memorial, and to the left the prominent

Norton Sub Hamdon

tower of Norton Sub Hamdon church. Go through the kissing gate, walk along the right edge of a field, go through a second kissing gate and bear left to head diagonally across to another one. Go through that, continue in the same direction across the next field and go through a metal gate in the far corner on to a track.

Turn left and at a fork a few yards ahead, take the right-hand hedge-lined path, signposted to Ham Hill. Go through two kissing gates in quick succession, walk uphill along the left edge of a field and go through another kissing gate in the field corner. Continue uphill through trees, ascend steps to a metal kissing gate, go through and turn right on to a steeper path. Go up more steps on to a tarmac drive, cross it and pass through a barrier opposite, at a public footpath sign to Ham Hill. Continue steeply up through woodland to a crossroads of paths **F**.

Turn left and walk along a clear, ridge top path, enjoying the superb views. At a fork, take the left-hand path to emerge from the trees and continue to a car park. Walk along the edge of it and keep ahead along an undulating path which descends to a road. Take the first turning on the right and follow the road round a right-hand bend to return to the start. ●

Cadbury Castle and the Corton Ridge

Start	Cadbury Castle
Distance	6½ miles (10.5km)
Approximate time	3 hours
Parking	Cadbury Castle, at south end of South Cadbury village
Refreshments	Pub at South Cadbury, pub at Corton Denham
Ordnance Survey maps	Landranger 183 (Yeovil & Frome), Pathfinder 1260, ST62/72 (Wincanton & Sparkford)

From a number of points on the walk there are outstanding views over the surrounding countryside. Foremost among these are Cadbury Castle, alleged site of King Arthur's Camelot; the slopes of Corton Hill; and, especially, the Corton ridge – a magnificent 1¼ mile (2km) ramble. The route passes through three attractive villages and the small amount of climbing involved is steady and relatively easy.

Turn right out of the car park and turn left up Castle Lane to Cadbury Castle. Go through a gate and continue along an enclosed, uphill track to reach the outer defences of this Iron Age fort.

The site of Arthur's court at Camelot (and, indeed, the very existence of the semi-mythical king himself) is among the greatest and most romantic mysteries of Dark Age Britain, but Cadbury Castle has a better claim than most. Excavations in the 1960s showed that the hill was extensively refortified around AD 500, about the time when a great British chieftain – possibly King Arthur – was leading the resistance to the Saxon advance in the south west. Whether or not this is Camelot, the site is an impressive one and the views from it are superb.

Retrace your steps downhill to the lane, turn left through South Cadbury, passing to the right of the medieval church, and at a crossroads in front of the Red Lion, turn left **A** along Folly Lane. The lane narrows, becomes an enclosed track and later continues along the right edge of a field, curving gradually left and with Cadbury Castle over to the left all the while.

Look out for where you turn right through a metal gate on to a narrow lane **B** and turn left along it into Sutton Montis, a small village whose church has a fine 13th-century tower and a Norman chancel arch. Pass to the left of the church and at a public footpath sign to Whitcombe and Corton Denham, turn left over a stile **C**. Walk along the right edge of a field, pass through a hedge gap, bear slightly right across an orchard and climb a stile on to a lane. Go through a metal gate opposite, climb a stile and head across a field to climb another on the far side. Ahead is a fine view of Corton Hill. Bear

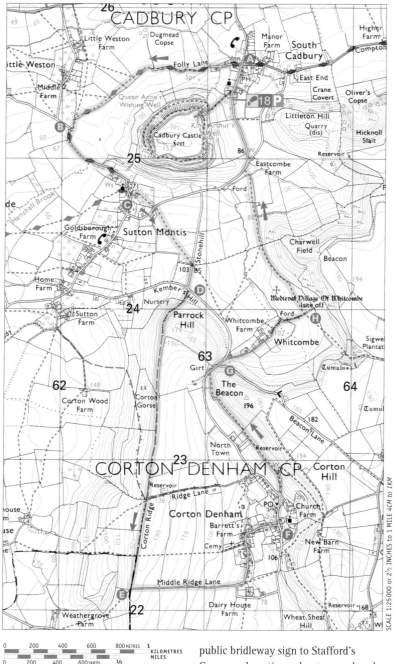

SCALE 1:25 000 or 2½ INCHES to 1 MILE 4CM to 1KM

| 0 | 200 | 400 | 600 | 800 METRES | 1 |
| 0 | 200 | 400 | 600 YARDS | ½ | |

KILOMETRES
MILES

slightly left to walk diagonally across
the next field and in the far corner
climb two stiles in quick succession on
to a lane.

Bear right to a T-junction **D**, turn
left and then immediately right, at a
public bridleway sign to Stafford's
Green, and continue along an enclosed
track to a gate. Go through to emerge
on to open grassland, turn right and
head uphill, soon bearing right on to a
clearer path which continues over
Parrock Hill on to the Corton ridge. Now
comes the most spectacular part of the
walk as you follow a broad, flat, grassy

Cadbury Castle – could this be Camelot?

path along the ridge. To the right are extensive views across the lush meadows and fertile farmlands of the Somerset Levels; to the left, in contrast, is the switchback profile of Corton Hill. Climb a stile, continue, go through a gate and keep ahead to a field corner where you turn left through a metal gate. Immediately turn right to go through another and continue along the ridge as far as a footpath post **E**.

Here turn left through a metal gate on to a straight, enclosed, hedge-lined track – Middle Ridge Lane – which heads steadily downhill to emerge on to a lane. Keep ahead, following the lane around two bends – first to the left, then to the right – through the village of Corton Denham, then head gently uphill to a T-junction in front of the Victorian church **F**.

Turn left and where the road curves left, bear right, at a public footpath sign to Whitcombe and Corton Hill, along an uphill, sunken, enclosed track. At a fork continue along the left-hand track to a metal gate, go through and keep ahead, slightly above and parallel to the left field edge, to a stile. Climb it and continue, by a wire fence on the left, contouring along the side of Corton Hill. Where the wire fence ends, descend slightly to continue by a line of trees on the left, and just before the field corner, bear left through a gap in the trees along a downhill path. After curving right, turn left over a stile and descend steps to a lane opposite a cottage.

Turn right, take the second turning on the right **G**, signposted Witcomb Farm Lane, and walk along a narrow lane. After passing a farm, the lane continues as a rough track. Bear right to ford a brook and head gently uphill along a tree-lined track to a T-junction of tracks **H**. The bumps in the ground ahead mark the site of the medieval village of Whitcombe (not to be confused with the other medieval village, Witcombe, on the route of walk 17). Turn left along the right edge of a field, by a wire fence on the right – Cadbury Castle lies immediately ahead – later keeping below an embankment on the right to reach a metal gate. Go through, keep ahead, by a line of trees on the right, and in the field corner turn right over a stile and go through a hedge gap on to a track.

Turn left, continue along the right edge of the field ahead and in the corner keep ahead to cross a footbridge over a brook. Continue across the next field and climb a stile on to a lane. Turn right, at a fork take the left-hand lane and follow it back to the start. ●

Hinton Charterhouse and Wellow

Start	Parking area off the A36 between Bath and Warminster opposite junction of lane to Hinton Charterhouse and Wellow
Distance	7 miles (11.3km)
Approximate time	3½ hours
Parking	Parking area off the A36
Refreshments	Pubs at Hinton Charterhouse, pub at Wellow
Ordnance Survey maps	Landranger 172 (Bristol & Bath), Explorer 5 (Mendip Hills East)

The walk starts by heading across fields to Hinton Charterhouse and then follows an attractive, undulating circular route between Hinton Charterhouse and Wellow. There are fine views, attractive wooded areas and some pleasant walking beside Wellow Brook. There are also plenty of 'ups and downs' but these are long and steady rather than steep and strenuous. Some of the enclosed tracks and lower level paths may be muddy after wet weather.

From the parking area cross the main road and take the lane opposite, signposted to Hinton Charterhouse and Wellow. At a public footpath sign turn left over a stile Ⓐ, walk across a field, climb another stile and keep ahead across the next field towards Hinton Charterhouse church. To the right is a fine view of the 18th-century Hinton House. Climb a stile, go through a kissing gate into the churchyard, pass to the left of the 13th-century church, turn left through a metal gate and keep ahead to a lane.

Turn right into the village of Hinton Charterhouse. At a crossroads by the Rose

and Crown Ⓑ, keep ahead along a lane, signposted as a No Through Road. After passing public footpath and bridleway signs, this continues as an enclosed track which gently descends to a stile.

Descending the lane into Wellow

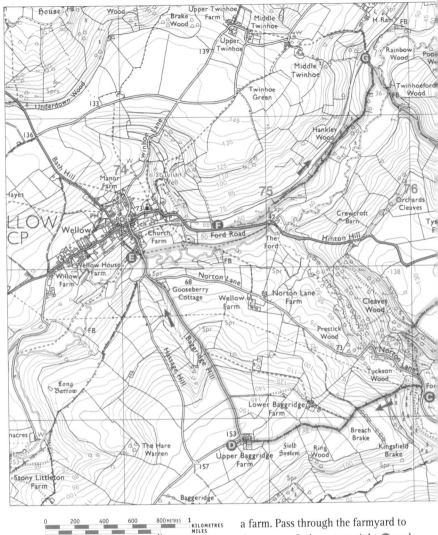

Climb it, at a fork keep ahead along the left-hand track which turns left into woodland, and at the next fork take the right-hand track. Keep right again at the next fork to continue along a narrow path down to a stile. Climb it, turn left along a lane and after 100 yds (91m), turn sharp right **C**, at a public footpath sign.

Cross a footbridge over Norton Brook and follow a track steadily uphill through woodland. Go through a metal gate and keep ahead along an enclosed track, going through a series of gates, to a farm. Pass through the farmyard to the corner of a lane, turn right **D** and continue downhill along this quiet, narrow lane, with fine views ahead of Wellow church and the line of hills beyond. Later descend more steeply and cross a footbridge over Wellow Brook by a ford **E**.

Keep ahead into the village if you wish to visit the pub and restored medieval church. Otherwise turn right over a stile, at a public footpath sign, and continue across meadows, climbing a series of stiles and keeping parallel to the winding brook. Finally bear left across the end of a meadow and climb a stile on to a road to the left of a cottage.

Turn left and after about 200 yds (183m) – on the brow of a hill – turn sharp right **F** along a grassy path to a gate. Go through, head diagonally across a field, go through a metal gate in the far corner and keep ahead along the top edge of the next field. Bear right across the narrow end of the field and go through a metal gate in the right-hand corner. Continue through woodland, go through a gate to emerge from the trees and head gently downhill along an enclosed path. In front of two metal gates turn right **G** along the left edge of a field, by Wellow Brook on the left, then turn left to cross two footbridges – the first over the brook itself and the second over another, more minor brook.

Turn right along a path through woodland, recross the minor brook, go through a gate and continue through an attractive narrow valley. Keep along the left edge of a succession of fields and go through a series of gates, ascending gently all the while. Eventually go through a gate in the last field corner on to a track.

Keep ahead between houses and continue uphill along a tarmac track into Hinton Charterhouse. At a crossroads just to the north of the outward route **H**, keep ahead along a lane for ¾ mile (1.2km) to return to the start. ●

Bradford-On-Avon, Westwood and Avoncliff

Start	Bradford-on-Avon
Distance	7 miles (11.3km)
Approximate time	3½ hours
Parking	Bradford-on-Avon
Refreshments	Pubs and cafés at Bradford-on-Avon, pub at Westwood, pub at Avoncliff
Ordnance Survey maps	Landrangers 172 (Bristol & Bath) and 173 (Swindon & Devizes), Pathfinders 1184, ST86/96 (Melksham) and 1200, ST85/95 (Westbury & Trowbridge)

This is a walk of great interest, scenic beauty and variety. It includes attractive waterside stretches along the banks of the rivers Avon and Frome and the Kennet and Avon Canal, farmland, woodland and superb views over both the Frome and Avon valleys. Historic interest is provided by the Saxon church, bridge chapel and tithe barn at Bradford-on-Avon, church and manor at Westwood, ruins of Farleigh Hungerford Castle (which involves a short detour), and the aqueduct at Avoncliff. Some muddy stretches can be expected. Allow plenty of time in order to enjoy this absorbing walk to the full.

Wool is a common link between Bradford-on-Avon and its larger Yorkshire namesake but there the similarity ends. While the northern Bradford expanded into a major industrial city during the Victorian era, Bradford-on-Avon declined, though the imposing 19th-century Abbey Mill would not look out of place in a Pennine valley. The result of this decline is a highly attractive town, sloping steeply down the sides of the valley to the river, with many fine stone buildings belonging to the 16th, 17th and 18th centuries, the heyday of the local Cotswold woollen trade.

The oldest building is the tiny Saxon church, a striking contrast to the imposing medieval church nearby. Built in the 10th century or even earlier, it is one of the best preserved Anglo-Saxon churches in England and was only rediscovered in the 19th century, having been used as a cottage and schoolroom. The medieval Town Bridge over the Avon has a rare chapel on it, later used as a lock up; the walk starts on the south side of this bridge.

Walk away from the bridge, passing the War Memorial gardens on the right, and turn right, at a footpath sign 'Saxon Church', into a car park. Turn left in front of St Margaret's Hall and take the paved riverside path, passing to the right of the Riverside Inn, to follow a pleasant wooded stretch of the Avon.

Pass under a railway bridge and at a T-junction turn right along a tarmac track through Barton Farm Country Park, a thin strip of land between river and canal that extends from Bradford to Avoncliff. Over to the left is the magnificent tithe barn, 168ft (51m) long, built in the 14th century to store produce for the nuns of Shaftesbury Abbey. Keep beside the river and after ¹/₂ mile (800m), the track bears left uphill to cross a footbridge over the Kennet and Avon Canal Ⓐ. Turn right beside the canal – this path may be muddy – climb two stiles in quick succession, continue along the right edge of a field and cross a footbridge in the field corner. Bear slightly left away from the canal and head uphill across the next field towards trees. Do not go

The River Avon at Bradford-on-Avon

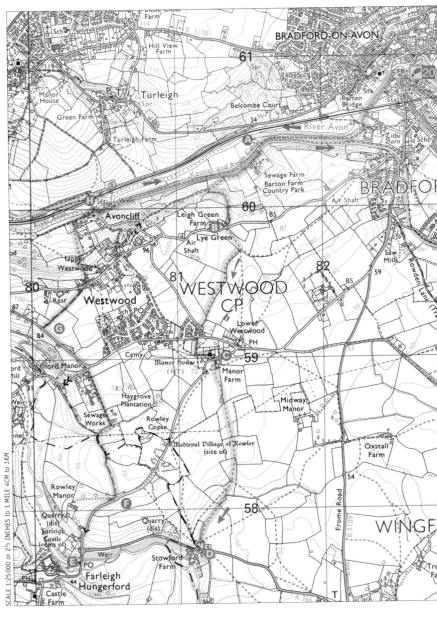

SCALE 1:25 000 or 2½ INCHES to 1 MILE 4CM to 1KM

through a metal kissing gate into the trees but turn sharp left and continue along the top edge of the field. From here there is a good view over the town. Pass through a hedge gap, continue to a stile, climb it and keep by a hedge and wire fence on the right. Climb another stile, keep ahead to climb yet another, at

a wall corner, and walk along a narrow, enclosed path. Go through a gate, continue to the left of a cottage and go through another gate on to a lane **B**.

Cross over, climb a stile and walk across a field, bearing left to keep alongside a hedge on the right. About 50 yds (46m) before the field corner you reach two stiles on the right; climb the first of these and continue along the left edge of fields, by a hedge on the left, climbing several stiles and eventually emerging on to a lane at Westwood. Continue along the lane to a T-junction, cross over, go up steps, through a kissing gate and walk along an enclosed path. Turn left into the churchyard, continue through it and go through a metal gate on to a lane **G**.

The dominant feature of Westwood's mainly 15th-century church is the tall west tower. To the left is Westwood Manor, also 15th-century but with Tudor and Jacobean additions. It is now owned by the National Trust. Further along the lane to the left is the pub.

Climb a metal stile opposite, head straight across a field, following the direction of a public footpath sign to Stowford, pass to the left of a circular, tree-fringed pond and go through a gap to continue across the next field. Climb a stile, continue across the next field, climb another stile and bear right across a field to a fence corner. Keep ahead to join a track, follow it down to a farm and go through a metal gate on to a road **D**. Turn right, turn left along the drive to Stowford Manor Farm and immediately turn right to head across grass to a stile. The next part of the route is along a permissive path. Climb the stile and continue across a series of narrow fields, between the road on the right and the River Frome on the left, eventually climbing a stile on to a road to the right of a bridge **E**.

The route continues to the right but turn left uphill if you wish to make a brief detour to visit Farleigh Hungerford Castle. This was built in the late 14th-century by Sir Thomas Hungerford and was later extended, taking over the entire village in the process. The Hungerfords built a new village and church, with the old church becoming the castle chapel.

On emerging on to the road turn right, not along the main road which curves to the right but along a narrow, uphill lane. Opposite a small layby, turn left **F** on to a track through trees to a metal gate. Go through and continue along this pleasant, enclosed track from which there are fine views to the left over the Frome valley. Later the track becomes tree-lined and descends to a stream. Turn right over a stile, walk along the bottom edge of a field parallel to the stream, turn left over it and go through a metal gate. Continue along the path ahead which soon joins a track and heads steadily uphill to a lane. Turn right to a T-junction and turn left along a road. To the left are Iford Manor Gardens, which are open to the public at various times.

After ¼ mile (400m) turn right **G**, at a public bridleway sign to Upper Westwood, along a hedge-lined path to a road. Turn right and after a few yards turn left along a track between houses to a stile. Ahead is a glorious view over the Avon valley. Climb the stile, head downhill along the right edge of a field and in the field corner turn right over a stile into trees. A few yards ahead turn sharp left, do not climb the stile in front but follow the path to the right and head down to climb a stile into a field. Continue downhill, making for a stile in the bottom right-hand corner, climb it and walk along a track by a wall on the right. Follow the track into Avoncliff and the river is below on the left.

Pass under the Avoncliff Aqueduct, which was built by John Rennie in 1810 to take the canal across the Avon valley, then head up to the pub and turn sharp right up to the aqueduct **H**. Turn left, here re-entering Barton Farm Country Park, and follow the quiet, tree-lined towpath back to Bradford-on-Avon. At the first footbridge **A** you rejoin the outward route – bear left down the tarmac track to the river and retrace your steps to the start. ●

Pewsey Downs

Start	Walkers Hill, car park at the top of the hill on the road between Alton Barnes and Lockeridge
Distance	7 miles (11.3km)
Approximate time	3½ hours
Parking	Walkers Hill
Refreshments	Pub at Honeystreet
Ordnance Survey maps	Landranger 173 (Swindon & Devizes), Pathfinder 1185, SU06/16 (Devizes & Marlborough)

The first part of the walk descends from Walkers Hill, high up on the Pewsey Downs overlooking the Vale of Pewsey, and passes through the adjoining hamlets of Alton Priors and Alton Barnes, both with ancient churches, to the Kennet and Avon Canal at Honeystreet. After a walk along the canal, the route continues into Stanton St Bernard and then ascends Milk Hill. On the final exhilarating downland stretch there are more grand views over the vale. The climb back on to the downs is gradual but with one fairly steep section.

From the car park cross the road and climb the stile opposite. Immediately turn left over another stile and walk across the grass, initially by a wire fence bordering the road on the left, later veering slightly right to a stile. Climb it and head uphill across the down, passing to the left of tumuli and close to Adam's Grave, a prehistoric long barrow which the Saxons called Woden's Barrow. At the top bear left and descend a worn grassy path to a stile. In front are glorious views over the Vale of Pewsey.

Climb the stile, here leaving Pewsey Down Nature Reserve, continue down a path to the road, turn left uphill and after 200 yds (183m), turn sharp right over a stile Ⓐ. This stile is beside a gate and quite difficult to spot. Walk along the right edge of a field and at a gap in the hedge on the right, bear slightly right to continue downhill along a sunken, enclosed, tree-lined path, which is likely to be muddy and overgrown. Later continue along a tarmac track to emerge on to a road in the hamlet of Alton Priors. Turn left, immediately turn right Ⓑ along a lane, and where it ends bear right through a wooden turnstile – the first of several on the next stage of the walk.

Keep along the left edge of a field, passing Alton Priors church on the left. This mainly dates from the 14th century but the interior is dominated by the fine Norman chancel arch. Continue along a paved path, go through a turnstile, cross two footbridges in quick succession and go through another turnstile. Keep by a wire fence on the left, bear left to follow the paved path diagonally across a field and go through the last of the turnstiles on to a lane in Alton Barnes. To the left

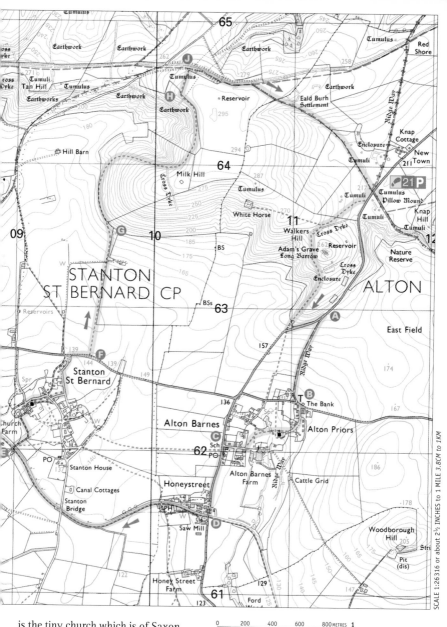

is the tiny church which is of Saxon origin, restored by the Victorians.

The route continues to the right along the lane to a T-junction **C**. Here turn left along the road into the canal settlement of Honeystreet, which was built in 1811 just after the opening of the Kennet and Avon canal. Remains of the wharf can still be seen. Cross the canal bridge, immediately turn right **D** to descend to the towpath and walk

along it, passing the Barge Inn. Over to the right the White Horse of Alton Barnes, which dates from 1812, can be seen on the side of the downs. At the second bridge, turn left in front of it, head up to a track and turn right **E** to cross the bridge. Follow the track to the left and, in front of Riding School buildings, turn first right and then left to reach a lane at a bend. Turn right through the village of Stanton St Bernard, passing to the left of the church – mainly 19th-century except for the medieval tower – and follow the lane around right- and left-hand bends to a T-junction.

Turn left and, at the next T-junction, turn right along a road. At a public footpath sign and White Horse waymark, turn left along the left-hand edge of a field, by a wire fence on the left. Cross a track and continue along the right-hand edge of a field to climb a waymarked stile. Turn left and keep along the bottom edge of the down, by a wire fence on the left which gradually curves to the right. Just before reaching the field corner, bear right and head steadily uphill, by a wire fence on the left. Turn left over a stile, continue more steeply uphill, now with

the wire fence on the right, and where that fence bends to the right, bear left and head across to a gate.

Go through and walk along a grassy track, by a wire fence on the right, curving gradually left over Milk Hill – at 963ft (294m) one of the highest points in Wiltshire. The views to the left across rolling downland are superb. Look out for where you turn right through a gate and keep beside a wire fence on the right to go through another. Turn right , and walk along a bridleway between a fence on the right and the Wansdyke on the left. This great earthwork is though to have been constructed in the 6th or 7th centuries by the Britons as a defence against the invading Anglo-Saxons.

At a junction with another bridleway, turn right onto it and head steadily downhill, by a wire fence on the right, climbing two stiles. Finally climb a third stile on to a road and the car park is directly opposite.

The White Horse of Alton Barnes from the canal

Stonehenge

Start	Amesbury, Recreation Ground car park at the end of Recreaton Road just across the bridge over the River Avon
Distance	8 miles (12.9km)
Approximate time	4 hours
Parking	Recreation Ground car park at Amesbury
Refreshments	Pubs and cafés at Amesbury, refreshment kiosk at Stonehenge
Ordnance Survey maps	Landranger 184 (Salisbury & The Plain), Pathfinders 1221, SU04/14 (Shrewton & Amesbury) and 1241, SU03/13 (Salisbury (North))

The highlight of this walk is the sudden view of Stonehenge ahead, dominating the skyline of Salisbury Plain and approached on foot across the downs, from where its location can be fully appreciated. Although the great monument is obviously the major focal point, there is much else to enjoy: the fine medieval church at Amesbury, extensive views across the downs and Avon valley, lush riverside meadows, and the numerous smaller prehistoric remains that lie within the vicinity of Stonehenge.

Amesbury is attractively situated on the River Avon which does a great loop to the south-west of the town. The church, with its Norman nave and 13th-century central tower, is unusually imposing. This is because it was probably the church of a medieval nunnery that stood nearby. After the dissolution of the monasteries in the 1530s, a house, Amesbury Abbey, was built on the site, and subsequently rebuilt in the 19th century. It is privately owned and not open to the public.

The walk begins just before the entrance to the Recreation Ground car park. Take the enclosed, tarmac path which heads down to cross two footbridges, the first one over a stream and the second over the River Avon. Continue along a path which bears right

to a crossroads of paths and a footpath post. Keep ahead, in the Durnford and 'Stonehenge Walk' direction, along a steadily ascending, enclosed track. At a crossroads keep ahead over the crest of the hill and then descend gently, with fine views to the right over the Avon valley, to a dip where the track forks.

Take the right-hand track, go through a metal kissing gate a few yards ahead and turn right **A**, at public footpath and 'Stonehenge Walk' signs, along the right edge of a field. In the field corner – near a chalk pit on the left – turn left along the bottom edge of the field, keep above a channel on the right, through a wooded area, then turn right over a footbridge. Continue along a winding path through trees – this part of the walk might be overgrown in the summer – and cross a footbridge over the Avon. Keep ahead over a ditch and continue along the left edge of a field to a stile. Climb it and turn right along a tarmac drive on to a lane in the hamlet of Normanton Ⓑ.

Turn left and just before reaching the medieval church at Wilsford, turn right Ⓒ on to the tarmac drive to Springbottom Farm. After a few yards bear right off the drive and continue steadily uphill along a most attractive, tree-lined path. The path later descends gently and at the bottom bear left to rejoin the drive, which bears left and then curves gradually right, passing to the left of the farm buildings. It then continues as a rough track which peters out just before a fork. Continue along the right-hand, wide, grassy track which heads gently uphill towards the crest of the downs.

On reaching the crest, Stonehenge suddenly appears ahead in the distance, a stunning sight especially as the busy road that runs past it is temporarily hidden from view. Pass between the Normanton Down Barrows, a series of Bronze Age burial chambers that stretches for over $\frac{1}{2}$ mile (800m) along the top of this low ridge, and shortly afterwards turn left over a stile Ⓓ. Walk along the edge of a field, climb a stile in the field corner, at a National Trust waymark, and turn right along a track to the main A303. Cross over this busy road, keep along the track ahead to the A344 and turn right along it Ⓔ, passing the entrance to Stonehenge.

This is the most famous single prehistoric monument in Britain – possibly, indeed, in Europe. Mysteries abound and controversies rage about its purpose and construction, in particular why – and how – the smaller bluestones were brought all the way from the Preseli Hills in Pembrokeshire to be erected here. Although it looks

deceptively simple, Stonehenge is a complex monument and appears to have been built in three main phases over a period of around 1500 years. The first stage was the construction of a large circular bank and ditch around 3000 BC. Next, about a thousand years later, came the circles of bluestones, which were subsequently re-arranged. Finally the circle of giant sarsen boulders with lintels, the most striking feature of the monument, was completed around 1400 BC. Despite the crowds and the proximity of busy main roads, Stonehenge still manages to exert a powerful influence and one can

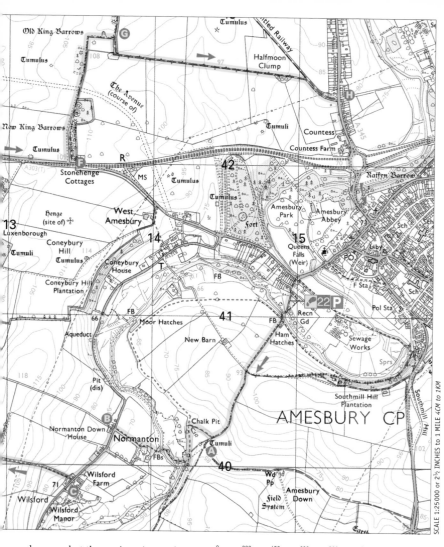

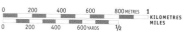

only marvel at the engineering and organisational skills that were needed for its construction.

Continue along the road – there is a cycle track on the right side – bear left on joining the A303 and, on reaching a belt of trees, turn left on to a track **F**. Go through a gate and continue along this pleasant enclosed track, alongside a line of impressive ancient beeches. More burial chambers are seen on this stage of the walk. In the woodland on the right there is the group known as the New King Barrows, and where the track later turns right it passes by the Old King Barrows.

Shortly after turning right you reach a T-junction **G**. Turn right, follow the track around a left bend and continue in a straight line for ¾ mile (1.2km), eventually bearing right to a road **H**. Turn right, keep ahead at a roundabout into Amesbury and take the first turning on the right (High Street). Continue along Church Street, passing to the left of the church, and cross the River Avon. Where the road bends right, turn left, at a public footpath sign, along Recreation Road to the start. ●

Cheddar Gorge

Start	Cheddar
Distance	5 miles (8km)
Approximate time	3 hours
Parking	Cheddar, Cliff Street car park
Refreshments	Pubs and cafés at Cheddar
Ordnance Survey maps	Landranger 182 (Weston-super-Mare & Bridgwater), Explorer 4 (Mendip Hills West)

Cheddar Gorge, a 450ft (137m) deep, 1 mile (1.6km) long chasm in the Mendip Hills, is one of the great natural wonders of Britain and this walk enables you to appreciate it at its best. A long, steady and at times steep climb along its north side, much of it through woodland, leads on to the fresh and open expanses of the Mendip plateau. After a descent there is a lovely stretch through a rocky, steep-sided, limestone valley, followed by another climb. Finally comes an exhilarating walk along the south rim of the gorge, with dramatic views down into it – be careful, there are some sheer drops – and extensive views over the Mendips and across the Somerset Levels.

To most people Cheddar is associated with cheese, gorge and caves. Cheese has been made in the area since at least the 12th century. The dramatic scenery of the gorge, coupled with the caves that honeycomb the limestone cliffs, have made the town a popular tourist resort with a multitude of gift shops, cafés, pubs and restaurants. But there is an older Cheddar as well. The Saxon kings of Wessex built a palace here, there is an impressive 14th- to 15th-century church with a tower 110ft (34m) high, and an old market cross in the town centre.

The walk begins at the bottom of the gorge at the road junction by Cliff Street car park. Walk along the road towards the gorge, passing the Butchers Arms on the right, and at a public footpath sign 'Gorge and Toilets' turn left on to a tarmac path **A**. The path swings right, later bends left, and at a public footpath sign continue uphill through trees along the side of the gorge, keeping parallel to the road and passing waterfalls.

On rejoining the road, immediately turn sharp left, at a public footpath sign, along an uphill track. Just after it flattens out, turn right and continue uphill along a narrow, enclosed path. The path turns left and continues up – where it emerges from the enclosed section, to the right of a house, turn sharp right **B**, almost doubling back, on to a steeply ascending path that winds through woodland. Climb a stile, keep ahead, turn right through a kissing gate in the wall on the right and turn left to continue up through trees, now with the wall on the left. Bear left to

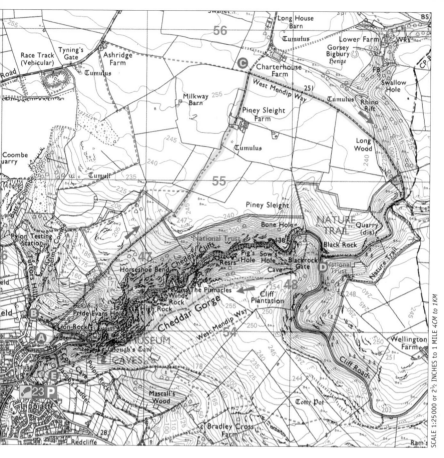

climb a stile in a wall corner, keep ahead for a few yards and turn right, now by the wall on the right again. Continue uphill through a mixture of scrub, gorse and trees and finally climb a stone stile at the top, by a wall corner, to emerge on to the Mendip plateau. The views over the Mendips and looking back to Cheddar and the reservoir beyond are superb.

Continue along the left edge of a series of fields, negotiating several gates and stiles and keeping parallel to a wall on the left. After climbing a stile, keep to the left of a farm, go through a gate and walk along a track. At a public footpath sign by a cattlegrid, turn right **C**, here joining the West Mendip Way, and continue along the right edge of fields. Climb two stiles, entering woodland after the second one. Descend

through the trees and climb a stile at the bottom – now comes a particulary attractive part of the walk as you continue through a steep-sided, dry, limestone valley with rocky outcrops, reminiscent of parts of the Yorkshire Dales and Peak District. It is part of the Black Rock Nature Reserve. After the track bends right, the valley becomes more wooded. Continue through it, climb a stile and finally go through a kissing gate on to a road **D**.

Climb the stile opposite and take the steep, rocky uphill path ahead through woodland. Go through a gate at the top, keep ahead and at a fork take the right-hand track, following the direction of the public bridleway sign, to continue

through trees and bracken to a stile.
Climb it and at another fork continue
along the left-hand path, by a wire
fence on the left, to the top of the gorge.

Now comes a succession of
spectacular views as you follow a path
along the rim of the gorge, with some
steep drops on the right, winding
steadily downhill through scrub and
trees and keeping to the main path all
the while. The cliffs lining the gorge are
so sheer that the road at the bottom is
not visible. Ahead the views extend

across Cheddar Reservoir and the
Somerset Levels to the coast and
Quantocks on the horizon.

Just before reaching Jacob's Tower,
opened in 1908, turn right **E** down
Jacob's Ladder, a long flight of steps –
nearly 300 – through woodland that
lines the side of the gorge. At the
bottom turn left along the road to
return to the start.

_Cheddar Reservoir and the Somerset Levels make
a magnificent backdrop to the Gorge and town._

Tollard Royal and Win Green

Start	Tollard Royal
Distance	7 miles (11.3km)
Approximate time	3½ hours
Parking	By village pond at Tollard Royal
Refreshments	Pub at Tollard Royal
Ordnance Survey maps	Landranger 184 (Salisbury & The Plain), Pathfinders 1261, ST82/92 (Shaftesbury) and 1281, ST81/91 (Shillingstone & Tollard Royal)

From the village of Tollard Royal near the Dorset border, several wooded valleys lead up on to a ridge. This route takes one of these, climbing steadily and quite steeply at times, to reach Win Green hill – at 911ft (277m) the highest point on Cranborne Chase and a magnificent vantage point. This is followed by a splendid ridge walk, with more outstanding views, and a descent via a parallel valley to return to the start.

Close to the medieval church in Tollard Royal is King John's House – originally a 13th-century hunting lodge, it was remodelled in the 16th century and restored during the Victorian era. Its name indicates that Cranborne Chase, an area of wooded valleys and rolling chalk uplands on the borders of Wiltshire and Dorset, was originally a royal forest – a favourite hunting ground of King John and other medieval monarchs. It became a private chase in the early 17th century when James I bestowed it upon Robert Cecil, Earl of Salisbury.

Start by taking the tarmac track to the left of the pond and, at a fork, continue along the left-hand track, following a Wessex Ridgeway sign. The track heads steadily uphill, enclosed by trees, to a stile. Climb it, continue by a wire fence on the left and after going through a metal gate, the track descends and bends left.

In front of a metal gate turn right over a stile, head across to climb another and turn right Ⓐ along a track that continues through Ashcombe Bottom. At a fork, take the left-hand track and before reaching a metal gate in front, bear left across grass and climb a stile, at public footpath and Wessex Ridgeway signs. Continue along a grassy track through trees, soon emerging into the open, pass to the right of a cottage and keep ahead, by a wire fence on the right. Where the grassy track ends, bear slightly right to continue along a broad, rough track.

On the next part of the walk there are three forks in fairly quick succession; in each case you take the left-hand track, following a series of red-topped metal footpath posts. The track now ascends steeply, bends left and continues uphill through woodland. Where the main track bends right, keep ahead **B** uphill through the trees to emerge on to open grassland. Continue uphill, passing a waymarked post, and later bear slightly left to keep alongside a wire fence on the right. Turn right over a stile in that fence and head across to the triangulation pillar and toposcope on the top of Win Green hill, 911ft (277m) **C**. From here, the highest point on Cranborne Chase, the magnificent all-round views extend across the wooded slopes of the chase to the Mendips, Marlborough Downs, New Forest, Dorset coast and even the Isle of Wight.

Walk past the triangulation pillar, passing to the left of a tree-encircled tumulus, and bear right around the curve of the tumulus to continue along a grassy downhill track. Bear right on joining a main track – there now follows an exhilarating ridge top walk, with superb views ahead and on both sides. At a junction of tracks bear left, ignoring a Byway sign to Tollard Royal, and the track skirts woodland on the right to join a narrow lane **D**. Keep along it for nearly ³/₄ mile (1.2km), still along the ridge top and with conifer woodland to the right. Opposite a lane to Berwick St John on the left, turn right on to a broad, clear track **E**.

After passing through the narrow belt of conifers, the track descends steadily, enclosed by fences. Where it ends, keep straight ahead across a large field, making for the right edge of the trees in front. At the far end of the field, go through a gap, cross a track, go through a metal gate and immediately turn left along the edge of a field. Follow the field edge to the right, continue gently downhill, skirting the right edge of

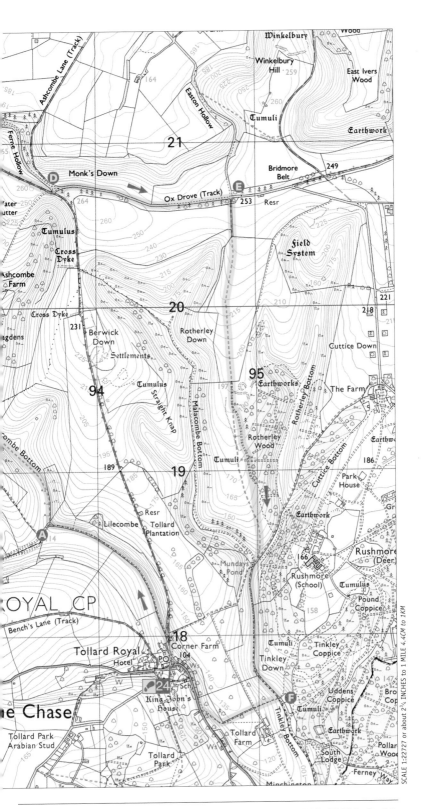

Rotherley Wood, and in the bottom corner follow the field edge to the right and turn left through a metal gate.

Descend along a grassy path to another metal gate, go through and continue through Tinkley Bottom, a delightful part of the walk. Go through a metal gate, continue through the valley bottom and just before reaching woodland – and in front of a metal gate – turn right **F** and follow a faint path uphill across grass to a waymarked stile.

Climb it, walk along a track, by a wire fence on the right, go through a metal gate and as you continue over the brow, the tower of Tollard Royal church can be seen over to the right among trees.

Where the wire fence turns right, continue along the track which bends right and heads downhill. Go through a metal gate on to a road and follow it back to the start.

The ridge path on Win Green hill

Barbury Castle and Ogbourne St Andrew

Start	Barbury Castle Country Park, signposted from B4005 to the east of Chiseldon
Distance	8½ miles (13.7km)
Approximate time	4 hours
Parking	Barbury Castle Country Park
Refreshments	Café at Country park, pub at Ogbourne St Andrew
Ordnance Survey maps	Landranger 173 (Swindon & Devizes), Pathfinder 1169, SU07/17 (Marlborough Downs)

From the superb viewpoint of Barbury Castle, a prehistoric hill fort high up on the Marlborough Downs, the route follows the Ridgeway down into the valley of the little River Og to the village of Ogbourne St Andrew. From here tracks lead back on to the open downs for an invigorating final stretch back to the fort. There are clear, broad tracks all the way, the views are extensive and all the gradients are gradual.

The walk begins on the Ridgeway – possibly the oldest routeway in Britain – which runs along the south side of the car park. Although the main part of the route lies to the left, first turn right, passing an information centre and going through a gate, to visit the earthworks of Barbury Castle, a large Iron Age fort defended by a double bank and ditches. The ditches enclose an area of 12½ acres (5.1 ha), and the site may have been re-fortified in Saxon times, as excavations have revealed evidence of a long period of occupation. As well as being impressive in its own right, the fort is also a magnificent viewpoint.

Retrace your steps to the car park and continue along the Ridgeway to a gate. Go through and turn right along a tarmac track which soon becomes a rough track. At a Ridgeway post turn

The Iron Age earthworks of Barbury Castle

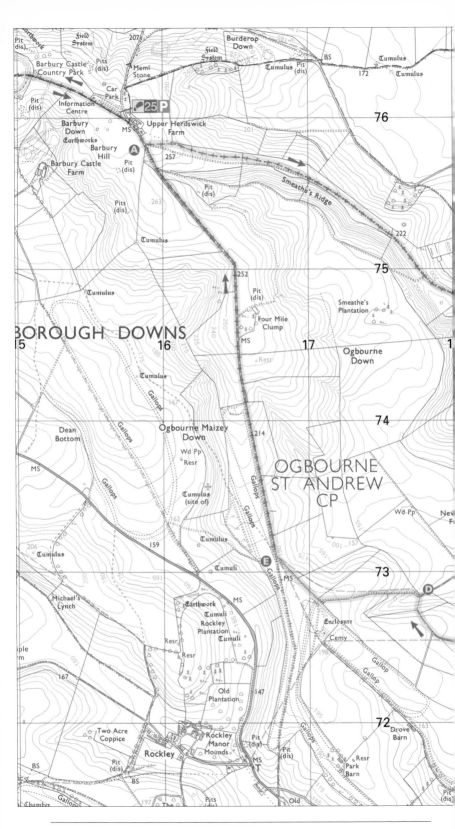

left **A** to follow a track across the downs, keeping along the top of Smeathe's Ridge. The views from here are superb. Go through a metal gate and after keeping by a wire fence on the right, look out for where waymarks direct you to bear left away from it.

Go through another metal gate, at a fork continue along the left-hand lower track, go through two more metal gates and eventually walk along an enclosed track which descends gently to a lane **B**. Turn right and where the lane bends left, keep ahead along an enclosed, tree-lined track. At a fingerpost where the enclosed section ends, continue ahead and soon the tower of Ogbourne St Andrew church comes into view, nestling at the foot of the down. Eventually the track emerges on to a lane. Turn right along it through the village, passing to the left of the medieval church, to a T-junction.

The pub is to the left but the route continues to the right **C** along a tarmac drive which after a few yards becomes a rough track. At a junction of tracks keep ahead, climbing gently back on to the downs. After descending, the track peters out – at this point bear right through a metal gate, head downhill across a field and at the bottom go through another metal gate on to a track **D**. Turn left and the track bends left and heads uphill towards a large barn on the skyline.

Pass to the right of this barn, climb a stile to the left of a gate and turn right along a track. On joining a broader track at a Byway sign, bear right along it **E** and follow it gently uphill across the broad downs. The track continues along the left inside edge of a group of trees, Four Mile Clump, and leads back to the start.

SCALE 1:25000 or 2½ INCHES to 1 MILE 4CM to 1KM

0	200	400	600	800 METRES	1
					KILOMETRES
					MILES
0	200	400	600 YARDS		½

Wells, Ebbor Gorge and Wookey Hole

Start	Wells
Distance	7½ miles (12.1km)
Approximate time	4 hours
Parking	Wells
Refreshments	Pubs and cafés at Wells, pub and cafés at Wookey Hole
Ordnance Survey maps	Landranger 182 (Weston-super-Mare & Bridgwater), Explorer 4 (Mendip Hills West)

Two of the major characteristics of the Mendip landscape, caves and a gorge, are featured on this walk, along with one of England's most beautiful cathedrals. Much of the route follows the West Mendip Way and the views from the higher points are superb. There is plenty of climbing, especially on the first part in order to get on to the Mendip plateau, and the final stretch gives fine views of Wells Cathedral. Make sure you leave plenty of time to explore the small but fascinating city of Wells.

Situated at the foot of the Mendips, Wells is the perfect English cathedral city. Not only is the cathedral, set in a spacious green close, one of the most beautiful in the country, but the group of ancillary buildings adjoining it are unrivalled. The cathedral mostly dates from the 13th century. Pride of place inevitably goes to the elaborate and striking west front, often considered the best of its kind, but the views of the east end are equally memorable. Inside, attention is drawn to the 14th-century inverted 'scissor' arches – a daring device introduced to support the central tower, which had begun to slip – and the unique double branching stairs leading to the chapter house. A great favourite with visitors is the clock in the north transept – every hour mounted knights stage a tournament around it.

To the south of the cathedral is the medieval bishop's palace, complete with walls, moat and a drawbridge. Leading off on the north side is the 14th-century Vicar's Close, which claims to be the oldest inhabited medieval street in Europe. It can be reached by a bridge from inside the cathedral.

The walk starts in the Market Place a few yards from the west front of the cathedral. Walk along Sadler Street, passing the Swan Hotel on the left, and at a T-junction turn right along New Street. Keep ahead at a fork, in the Bristol and Bath direction, and at a West Mendip Way notice, turn left along a tarmac track Ⓐ. Turn first right and then left to continue along Lovers Walk, then keep ahead along a hedge-lined, tarmac path, by school playing fields on the right.

SCALE 1:25 000 or 2½ INCHES to 1 MILE 4CM to 1KM

At a public footpath sign to Wookey Hole, the path bends right and continues in a straight line between playing fields and school buildings. It then keeps along the left edge of a field and heads gently uphill to go through a metal gate and on to a road. Cross over, take the enclosed tarmac path opposite, cross another road, continue uphill, go through a kissing gate and keep ahead to a lane **B**.

Turn sharp right and take the first turning on the left, Reservoir Lane. The

The west front of Wells Cathedral

lane continues as a rough track – where this bends left, keep ahead uphill along the right inside edge of woodland and bear right to a stile. Climb it, head diagonally across a field and go through a metal gate on to a road. Turn right downhill and where the road curves right, turn left **C**, at a public bridleway sign, along an uphill, enclosed, sunken path. This section may be muddy. The path later winds through woodland to a T-junction. Turn left downhill and continue along a tarmac drive to a road **D**. Turn right, head steeply uphill and at the top turn left along a track, at a Byway sign to Dursdon Drove **E**.

Most of the climbing is now over as you follow this old drove road for just over 1 mile (1.6km). Initially tree-lined, it bears right and continues as a wide, straight, enclosed track across the Mendip plateau. At the drive to Higher Pitts Farm turn left **F**, rejoining the West Mendip Way, bear right to pass to the right of the farm and bear left off the track to continue along a path in front of a house. The path bends left to a metal gate. Go through and keep along the right edge of the next three fields, going through another metal gate and climbing two stiles. The second stile admits you to the Ebbor Gorge National Nature Reserve. Head downhill between

gorse and scattered trees, climb a stile, turn left and continue downhill through woodland, passing two English Nature car park signs. At the second of these you turn left **G**, but a brief detour ahead brings you to the cliff edge and a magnificent view down the spectacular Ebbor Gorge.

After turning left descend by the side of the gorge, via a winding, stepped path through woodland, to a T-junction. Turn left, climb a stile and continue along the bottom of the gorge. The track curves right by a cottage to a metal gate. Go through and turn left **H** along the road through Wookey Hole, passing the entrance to the caves.

At the end of the village turn left through a kissing gate **J**, at a West Mendip Way sign, head uphill by a hedge along the right edge of a field and go through another kissing gate. Continue along an enclosed path, go through a kissing gate and turn left through a hedge gap. Walk uphill across the next field, skirting the edge of woodland on the left, and continue up to climb a stile in the far corner. Follow an uphill track through trees on to the open hilltop, from which the views are particularly fine, and head for the next group of trees. Here the path bears right and continues steeply downhill through woodland to a stile. Climb it, continue along the left edge of a field and go through a kissing gate. Keep ahead along a track and bear left on joining another track, by the huge Underwood Quarry on the right.

Descend to a junction of tracks by a footpath post and turn right along a tarmac drive, still alongside the quarry. At the next West Mendip Way post the drive bears left but you keep ahead along a track, rejoining the outward route. Retrace your steps to the start, enjoying grand views of the cathedral on the descent into Wells. ●

Savernake Forest

Start	Marlborough
Distance	10 miles (16.1km)
Approximate time	5 hours
Parking	Marlborough
Refreshments	Pubs and cafés at Marlborough
Ordnance Survey maps	Landrangers 173 (Swindon & Devizes) and 174 (Newbury & Wantage), Pathfinders 1185, SU06/16 (Devizes & Marlborough) and 1186, SU26/36 (Hungerford & Savernake Forest)

The first part of this highly attractive walk is along the Kennet valley to the east of Marlborough, between the Marlborough Downs and Savernake Forest. Most of the remainder is through the extensive woodlands and glades of the forest, survivals of an ancient royal hunting ground that once covered much of eastern Wiltshire. Although a lengthy walk, it is not particularly strenuous and there are no steep gradients, but expect some muddy footpaths in places.

Marlborough's long, unusually wide and handsome High Street reflects the town's importance throughout the centuries as a staging post on the main road from London to Bath and Bristol. A church stands at each end of it – at the west end is the 15th-century St Peter's and beyond that the buildings of Marlborough College. At the east end behind the Town Hall is St Mary's, mostly rebuilt in the Cromwellian period following the Great Fire of 1653 which destroyed much of the town and gutted the church, though it does retain a fine Norman doorway at the west end.

The walk starts at the east end of the High Street in front of the Town Hall, which was built between 1900 and 1902 on the site of its predecessor. Pass to the left of the Town Hall and follow the road to the left, then take the first turning on the right (Silverless Street).

Keep ahead at a crossroads by The Green, site of the original Saxon settlement of Marlborough, and continue along the road for ½ mile (800m). Just after crossing a bridge over the little River Og, bear right through a metal kissing gate, at a public footpath sign to Werg **A**.

Walk across a field to the right-hand edge and keep alongside a wire fence on the right. In the field corner go through a metal gate into woodland, climb a stile, ascend steps, cross a disused railway track **B** and descend steps on the other side. Bear right by trees along the right edge of a field, and at a corner turn right on to a track. The track soon curves left and continues along the right edge of fields. Climb a stile just to the left of a field corner, at a public footpath sign, head across a field to climb another and continue along a track between farm buildings. Turn left on to a tarmac drive, immediately turn right and after a few yards turn left up steps and go through a lych gate into Mildenhall (shortened locally to Minal) churchyard. Pass to the right of the church, a most attractive and interesting building which retains an impressive Norman nave and was extensively remodelled in the Georgian period.

Follow the path to the left and bear right to go through two kissing gates in quick succession. Walk across a field, keeping parallel to a wire fence on the right, go through a gate, turn first right and then left and continue along the right edge of the next field. Go through a metal gate, walk along the right edge of a cricket field and in the corner keep ahead along an enclosed path to a lane **C**.

Turn right, cross the River Kennet, then follow the narrow lane around right- and left-hand bends and head up to a T-junction. Turn left and at a fork ahead, take the right-hand, tarmac drive **D**. After passing in front of a bungalow, the drive becomes a rough track which heads uphill through trees. Cross a track, continue up to cross another and take the narrow, tree-lined path ahead (Cock-a-troop Lane) – this may be overgrown in places – then climb a stile to enter Savernake Forest.

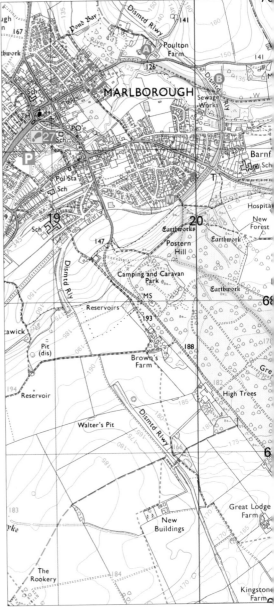

Originally a royal forest, in the 16th century Savernake passed into the ownership of the powerful Seymour family – it was here that Henry VIII courted his third wife, Jane Seymour – and at the end of the 17th century passed to the Bruces, later earls of Ailesbury. It is still owned by that family, but most of it is leased to the

Forestry Commission. Savernake is noted for its avenues, particularly the Grand Avenue, a great beech-lined drive planted by the 3rd Earl of Ailesbury in the 18th century.

Keep ahead to a public footpath sign and turn left along a track **E**. Pass beside a barrier and continue through a beautiful stretch of woodland, descending slightly to a lane. Turn right along it to the A4, turn right and after a few yards turn sharp left **F** along a straight forest track. The track heads gently uphill and then flattens out to reach a crossroads. Keep ahead, in the

Savernake Lodge direction, and just before the track emerges from the trees, turn right **G**. Pass beside a barrier, continue along a track and at the first crossroads turn left on to a grassy track. This track (Pig Stye) is indistinct in places but keep in a straight line and pass beside a barrier to a tarmac drive; this is the Grand Avenue. Cross it, pass beside another barrier and continue to a T-junction **H**.

Turn sharp right and walk along a track (Twelve O'Clock Drive) to Eight Walks, a junction of tracks about half-way along the Grand Avenue that radiate out with exact geometric precision, like the spokes of a wheel. Take the second track on the left **J** – a straight, wide track – and where it bends left after nearly 1 mile (1.6km), keep ahead beside a barrier along a rough track. About 100 yds (91m) before reaching a road, turn right **K** on

Savernake Forest

to a clear and distinct path (Church Walk) which gently descends to an open, grassy area. At a fork continue along the left-hand path, heading gently uphill across grass to re-enter trees, and at the next fork take the right-hand grassy track. Keep ahead at the first crossroads of tracks and continue downhill to a second crossroads. Here turn left **L** along a tarmac track (Long Harry), pass beside one barrier, then cross a track and pass beside another . After passing a third barrier, the track curves left across Postern Hill picnic site to a fork.

Take the right-hand track, which later bends right, keep along the right edge of an open area and then continue along a descending grassy track. From here there is a view to the left over Marlborough. Continue steeply downhill along the narrow path ahead, initially across scrub and later through a belt of trees, to a fence. At a sign 'Chisledon and Marlborough Railway Path' in front of the fence, turn right on to a track **M**, a walking and cycling route created from a disused railway.

Walk along the hedge-lined track which, after passing under a bridge, curves gradually left. The next section is beautifully tree-lined and there is a dramatic view as you cross a bridge high above the River Kennet. Continue through woodland and look out for wooden rails and steps on both sides of the track. Here turn left **B** down the steps, rejoining the outward route, and retrace your steps into Marlborough.

Burrington Combe, Dolebury Warren and Black Down

Start	Burrington Combe, car park opposite the Rock of Ages and beside the Burrington pub
Distance	8½ miles (13.7km) Shorter version 6 miles (9.7km)
Approximate time	4½ hours (3 hours for shorter walk)
Parking	Burrington Combe
Refreshments	Pub at start
Ordnance Survey maps	Landranger 182 (Weston-super-Mare & Bridgwater), Explorer 4 (Mendip Hills West)

Although this walk takes you to the highest point of the Mendips on Black Down, it is not a strenuous one as nearly all the climbs are gradual ones. Most of the route is through lovely woods and across open heathland, with superb views over the Mendips and, from the higher points, across to the Bristol Channel coast. The shorter version omits the National Trust area of Dolebury Warren, one of the fine viewpoints.

Burrington Combe is a deep ravine in the Mendips, almost as dramatic as the better known Cheddar Gorge to the south. Opposite the car park is the Rock of Ages, so called because a local 18th-century clergyman, Augustus Toplady, is supposed to have composed the hymn of that name while sheltering from a storm in a cleft in the rock. It is difficult to see how it could provide much shelter today.

From the car park turn right along the road, passing the pub and a garden centre, and bear left along a track. At a 'Road Used as a Public Path' sign in front of a house, turn left **Ⓐ** along a steeply ascending, enclosed path through trees to a narrow lane. Turn left, at a public footpath sign turn right on to a path, then climb a stile to enter Mendip Lodge Wood and bear right uphill – the track later flattens out.

About 50 yds (46m) before a ruined building, bear left along an uphill track and at a footpath post turn right down to a waymarked stile. Climb it, turn left and continue along an uphill, enclosed track under an avenue of trees as far as a waymarked stile on the right by a Woodland Trust notice **Ⓑ**.

*Here the shorter walk keeps ahead, rejoining the full walk at point **Ⓓ**.*

For the full walk climb the stile and continue along a path that initially keeps along the left inside edge of the woodland. Later head downhill along a winding track through the trees and, in front of a gate, turn left over a stile.

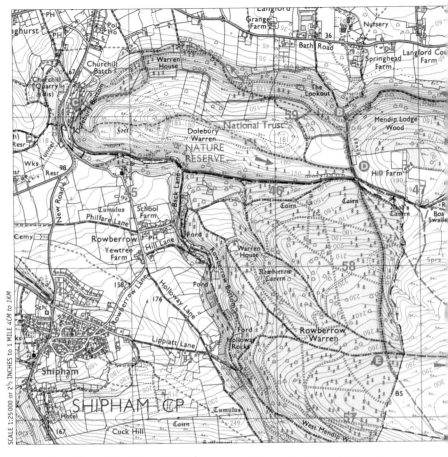

SCALE 1:25000 or 2½ INCHES to 1 MILE 4CM to 1KM

Pass in front of a house and continue along the path ahead to the corner of the wood where the path bears right to reach a stile.

Here turn left uphill along the right inside edge of the wood, cross one track and continue steadily uphill to a second. Cross that and bear slightly right to follow a winding, uphill path through thick woodland to a stile. Climb it, keep ahead through gorse and scrub and turn right along a clear path, heading downhill to climb a stile. At the T-junction ahead by a National Trust Dolebury Warren sign, turn left uphill **C**. The track first curves left, then bears right and continues across the extensive earthworks of a large Iron Age fort.

After passing through the outer ramparts, continue along a lovely, grassy ridge path, from which there are grand views on both sides, to a stile. Climb it, keep ahead through trees and at a Limestone Link sign, bear right and head downhill, curving right to another stile. Climb that, turn left and follow a grassy track across a field, by an intermittent line of trees on the right. Climb another stile, here leaving Dolebury Warren, to reach a T-junction and turn right **D**, here rejoining the shorter route.

Follow a track through woodland, keep ahead at a crossroads of tracks and bear right to another crossroads. Continue, passing a Forestry Commission Rowberrow Warren sign, along a broad, steadily ascending track. Keep ahead all the while and at the next

Batch, at 1067ft (325m) the highest point on the Mendips. Although it is not on a right of way, the Conservators who manage this area of common land have no objection to walkers making the brief diversion to the right in order to enjoy the magnificent view, provided that you keep to an obvious path. In clear weather the spectacular, panoramic view extends across the Mendips, the Somerset Levels and coast to the Quantocks and the hills of South Wales on the horizon.

Return to the track, head downhill to a T-junction, turn right and continue down to a junction of tracks and paths by a footpath post

crossroads turn left **E**, soon emerging from the trees on to the open heathland of Black Down.

Keep ahead across the down, crossing one track, and at the second one bear left along it **F**. The track passes just below the triangulation pillar at Beacon

Dolebury Warren

G. Turn sharp left and at a fork a few yards ahead, take the right-hand path to continue along the bottom edge of Black Down. Soon Burrington Combe can be seen over to the right. Descend into trees, turn sharp right to ford a brook and shortly afterwards descend to ford another one. Follow the path around a right bend, keep ahead past a public bridleway sign and continue uphill to a crossroads of tracks and paths by a footpath post **H**.

Turn right and head in a straight line across bracken. At times the path is difficult to follow and at other times a multitude of paths can be confusing, but keep ahead to emerge on to a track near a cottage. Turn right downhill through woodland and at a 'Road Used as a Public Path' sign, turn right again and retrace your steps to the start. ●

Further Information

 ## The National Trust

Anyone who likes visiting places of natural beauty and/or historic interest has cause to be grateful to the National Trust. Without it, many such places would probably have vanished by now.

It was in response to the pressures on the countryside posed by the relentless march of Victorian industrialisation that the trust was set up in 1895. Its founders, inspired by the common goals of protecting and conserving Britain's national heritage and widening public access to it, were Sir Robert Hunter, Octavia Hill and Canon Rawnsley: respectively a solicitor, a social reformer and a clergyman. The latter was particularly influential. As a canon of Carlisle Cathedral and vicar of Crosthwaite (near Keswick), he was concerned about threats to the Lake District and had already been active in protecting footpaths and promoting public access to open countryside. After the flooding of Thirlmere in 1879 to create a large reservoir, he became increasingly convinced that the only effective way to guarantee protection was outright ownership of land.

The purpose of the National Trust is to preserve areas of natural beauty and sites of historic interest by acquisition, holding them in trust for the nation and making them available for public access and enjoyment. Some of its properties have been acquired through purchase, but many have come to the Trust as donations. Nowadays, it is not only one of the biggest landowners in the country, but also one of the most active conservation charities, protecting 581,113 acres (253,176 ha) of land, including 555 miles (892km) of coastline, and over 300 historic properties in England, Wales and Northern Ireland. (There is a separate National Trust for Scotland, which was set up in 1931.)

Furthermore, once a piece of land has come under National Trust ownership, it is difficult for its status to be altered. As a result of parliamentary legislation in 1907, the Trust was given the right to declare its property inalienable, so ensuring that in any subsequent dispute it can appeal directly to parliament.

As it works towards its dual aims of conserving areas of attractive countryside and encouraging greater public access (not easy to reconcile in this age of mass tourism), the Trust provides an excellent service for walkers by creating new concessionary paths and waymarked trails, maintaining stiles and footbridges and combating the ever-increasing problem of footpath erosion.

For details of membership, contact the National Trust at the address on page 94.

 ## The Ramblers' Association

No organisation works more actively to protect and extend the rights and interests of walkers in the countryside than the Ramblers' Association. Its aims are clear: to foster a greater knowledge, love and care of the countryside; to assist in the protection and enhancement of public rights of way and areas of natural beauty; to work for greater public access to the countryside; and to encourage more people to take up rambling as a healthy, recreational leisure activity.

It was founded in 1935 when, following the setting up of a National Council of Ramblers' Federations in 1931, a number of federations earlier formed in London, Manchester, the Midlands and elsewhere came together to create a more effective pressure group, to deal with such problems as the disappearance and obstruction of footpaths, the prevention of access to open mountain and moorland and increasing hostility from landowners. This was the era of the mass trespasses, when there were sometimes violent confrontations between ramblers and gamekeepers, especially on the moorlands of the Peak District.

Since then the Ramblers' Association has played an influential role in preserving and developing the national footpath network, supporting the creation of national parks and encouraging the designation and waymarking of long-distance routes.

Our freedom to walk in the countryside is precarious and requires constant vigilance. As well as the perennial problems of footpaths being illegally obstructed, disappearing through lack of use or extinguished by housing or road construction, new dangers can spring up at any time.

It is to meet such problems and dangers that the Ramblers' Association exists and represents the interests of all walkers. The address to write to for information on the Ramblers' Association and how to become a member is given on page 94.

The address to write to for information on the Ramblers' Association and how to become a member is given on page 94.

Black Rock, near Cheddar

Walkers and the Law

The average walker in a national park or other popular walking area, armed with an Ordnance Survey map, reinforced perhaps by a guidebook giving detailed walking instructions, is unlikely to run into legal difficulties, but it is useful to know something about the law relating to public rights of way. The right to walk over certain parts of the countryside has developed over a long period, and how such rights came into being is a complex subject, too lengthy to be discussed here. The following comments are intended simply as a helpful guide, backed up by the Countryside Access Charter, a concise summary of walkers' rights and obligations drawn up by the Countryside Commission (see page 93).

Basically there are two main kinds of public rights of way: footpaths (for walkers only) and bridleways (for walkers, riders on horseback and pedal cyclists). Footpaths and bridleways are shown by broken green lines on Ordnance Survey Pathfinder and Outdoor Leisure maps and broken red lines on Landranger maps. There is also a third category, called byways: chiefly broad tracks (green lanes) or farm roads, which walkers, riders and cyclists have to share, usually only occasionally, with motor vehicles. Many of these public paths have been in existence for hundreds of years and some even originated as prehistoric trackways and have been in constant use for well over 2000 years. Ways known as RUPPs (roads used as public paths) still appear on some maps. The legal definition of such byways is ambiguous and they are gradually being reclassified as footpaths, bridleways or byways.

The term 'right of way' means exactly what it says. It gives right of passage over what, in the vast majority of cases, is private land, and you are required to keep to the line of the path and not stray on to the land on either side. If you inadvertently wander off the right of way – either because of faulty map-reading or because the route is not clearly indicated on the ground – you are technically trespassing and the wisest course is to ask the nearest available person (farmer or fellow walker) to direct you back to the correct route. There are stories about unpleasant confrontations between walkers and farmers at times, but in general most farmers are co-operative when responding to a genuine and polite request for assistance in route-finding.

Obstructions can sometimes be a problem and probably the most common of these is where a path across a field has been ploughed up. It is legal for a farmer to plough up a path provided that he restores it within two weeks, barring exceptionally bad weather. This does not always happen and here the walker is presented with a dilemma: to follow the line of the path, even if this inevitably means treading on crops, or to walk around the edge of the field. The latter course of action often seems the best but this means that you would be trespassing and not keeping to the exact line of the path. In the case of other obstructions which may block a path (illegal fences and locked gates etc), common sense has to be used in order to negotiate them by the

easiest method – detour or removal. You should only ever remove as much as is necessary to get through, and if you can easily go round the obstruction without causing any damage, then you should do so. If you have any problems negotiating rights of way, you should report the matter to the rights of way department of the relevant council, which will take action with the landowner concerned.

Apart from rights of way enshrined by law, there are a number of other paths available to walkers. Permissive or concessionary paths have been created where a landowner has given permission for the public to use a particular route across his land. The main problem with these is that, as they have been granted as a concession, there is no legal right to use them and therefore they can be extinguished at any time. In practice, many of these concessionary routes have been established on land owned either by large public bodies such as the Forestry Commission, or by a private one, such as the National Trust, and as these mainly encourage walkers to use their paths, they are unlikely to be closed unless a change of ownership occurs.

Walkers also have free access to country parks (except where requested to keep away from certain areas for

Stonehenge

Countryside Access Charter

Your rights of way are:

- public footpaths – on foot only. Sometimes waymarked in yellow
- bridle-ways – on foot, horseback and pedal cycle. Sometimes waymarked in blue
- byways (usually old roads), most 'roads used as public paths' and, of course, public roads – all traffic has the right of way

Use maps, signs and waymarks to check rights of way. Ordnance Survey Pathfinder and Landranger maps show most public rights of way

On rights of way you can:

- take a pram, pushchair or wheelchair if practicable
- take a dog (on a lead or under close control)
- take a short route round an illegal obstruction or remove it sufficiently to get past

You have a right to go for recreation to:

- public parks and open spaces – on foot
- most commons near older towns and cities – on foot and sometimes on horseback
- private land where the owner has a formal agreement with the local authority

In addition you can use the following by local or established custom or consent, but ask for advice if you are unsure:

- many areas of open country, such as moorland, fell and coastal areas, especially those in the care of the National Trust, and some commons
- some woods and forests, especially those owned by the Forestry Commission
- country parks and picnic sites
- most beaches
- canal towpaths
- some private paths and tracks Consent sometimes extends to horse-riding and cycling

For your information:

- county councils and London boroughs maintain and record rights of way, and register commons
- obstructions, dangerous animals, harassment and misleading signs on rights of way are illegal and you should report them to the county council
- paths across fields can be ploughed, but must normally be reinstated within two weeks
- landowners can require you to leave land to which you have no right of access
- motor vehicles are normally permitted only on roads, byways and some 'roads used as public paths'

ecological reasons, such as wildlife protection, woodland regeneration, safeguarding of rare plants etc), canal towpaths and most beaches. By custom, though not by right, you may generally walk across the open and uncultivated higher land of mountain, moorland and fell, but this varies from area to area and from one season to another – grouse moors, for example, will be out of bounds during the breeding and shooting seasons, and some open areas are used as Ministry of Defence firing ranges, for which reason access will be restricted. In some areas the situation has been clarified as a result of 'access agreements' between the landowners and either the county council or the national park authority, which

clearly define when and where you can walk over such open country.

Walking Safety

Although the reasonably gentle countryside that is the subject of this book offers no real dangers to walkers at any time of the year, it is still advisable to take sensible precautions and follow certain well-tried guidelines.

Always take with you both warm and waterproof clothing and sufficient food and drink. Wear suitable footwear, such as strong walking-boots or shoes that give a good grip over stony ground, on slippery slopes and in muddy conditions. Try to obtain a local weather forecast and bear it in mind before you start. Do not be afraid to abandon your proposed route and return to your starting point in the event of a sudden and unexpected deterioration in the weather.

All the walks described in this book will be safe to do, given due care and respect, even during the winter. Indeed, a crisp, fine winter day often provides perfect walking conditions, with firm ground underfoot and a clarity that is not possible to achieve at any other time of the year.

The most difficult hazard likely to be encountered is mud, especially when walking along woodland and field paths, farm tracks and bridleways – the latter in particular can often get churned up by cyclists and horses. In summer, an additional difficulty may be narrow and overgrown paths, particularly along the edges of cultivated fields. Neither should constitute a major problem provided that the appropriate footwear is worn.

 Useful Organisations

Council for the Protection of Rural England
Warwick House
25 Buckingham Palace Road
London SW1W 0PP
Tel. 0171 976 6433

Countryside Commission
John Dower House
Crescent Place
Cheltenham
Gloucestershire GL50 3RA
Tel. 01242 521381

Forestry Commission
Information Branch
231 Corstorphine Road
Edinburgh EH12 7AT
Tel. 0131 334 0303

Long Distance Walkers' Association
10 Temple Park Close, Leeds
West Yorkshire LS15 0JJ
Tel. 0113 264 2205

National Trust
Membership and general enquiries:
PO Box 39, Bromley, Kent BR1 3XL
Tel. 0181 315 1111
Wessex Regional Office:
Eastleigh Court, Bishopstrow
Warminster, Wiltshire, BA12 9HW
Tel. 01985 843600

Ordnance Survey
Romsey Road, Maybush,
Southampton SO16 4GU
Tel. 0345 330011 (Lo-call)

Ramblers' Association
1–5 Wandsworth Road
London SW8 2XX
Tel. 0171 582 6878

Tourist Information
West Country Tourist Board
60 St David's Hill
Exeter EX4 4SY
Tel. 01392 76351
Local tourist information offices:
(* not open all year)

Amesbury: 01980 622833
Bath: 01225 462831
Bradford-on-Avon: 01225 865797
Chard: 01460 67463
*Cheddar: 01934 744071
Chippenham: 01249 657733
Devizes: 01380 729408
Frome: 01373 467271
Glastonbury: 01458 832954
Marlborough: 01672 513989
Melksham: 01225 707424
Mere: 01747 861211
Minehead: 01643 702624
*Podimore: 01935 841302
Salisbury: 01722 334956
Shaftesbury: 01747 853514
Sherborne: 01935 815341
Swindon: 01793 530328
Taunton: 01823 336344
*Tetbury: 01666 503552
Trowbridge: 01225 777054
Warminster: 01985 218548
Wells: 01749 672552
Westbury: 01373 827158
Yeovil: 01935 71279

The Youth Hostels Association
Trevelyan House, 8 St Stephen's Hill
St Albans, Hertfordshire AL1 2DY
Tel. 01727 855215

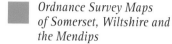

Ordnance Survey Maps of Somerset, Wiltshire and the Mendips

Somerset, Wiltshire and the Mendips are covered by Ordnance Survey 1:50 000 ($1\frac{1}{4}$ inches to 1 mile or 2cm to 1km) scale Landranger map sheets 172, 173, 174, 181, 182, 183, 184, 193, 194 and 195. These all-purpose maps are packed with useful information compiled to help you explore the area. In addition, they show viewpoints, picnic sites, places of interest and caravan and camping sites, as well as other information likely to be of interest.

To examine the Somerset, Wiltshire and Mendips area in more detail, and especially if you are planning walks, we recommend the following maps: Ordnance Survey Explorer map 4, Mendip Hills West, and Explorer map 5, Mendip Hills

East, at 1:25 000 ($2\frac{1}{2}$ inches to 1 mile or 4cm to 1km) scale.

The following Pathfinder maps, also at 1:25 000 scale, cover the area:

1154 (SU28/38)	1221 (SU04/14)
1166 (ST47/57)	1240 (ST83/93)
1168 (ST87/97)	1241 (SU03/13)
1169 (SU07/17)	1259 (ST42/52)
1170 (SU27/37)	1260 (ST62/72)
1181 (ST26/36)	1261 (ST82/92)
1183 (ST66/76)	1262 (SU02/12)
1184 (ST86/96)	1278 (ST21/31)
1185 (SU06/16)	1279 (ST41/51)
1186 (SU26/36)	1281 (ST81/91)
1200 (ST85/95)	

To get to the area, use the Ordnance Survey Great Britain Routeplanner (Travelmaster map number 1) at 1:625 000 scale (1 inch to 10 miles or 1cm to 6.25 km) or Travelmaster map 8 (South West England and South Wales) and Travelmaster map 9 (South East England including London) at 1:250 000 scale (1 inch to 4 miles or 1 cm to 2.5 km).

Ordnance Survey maps and guides are available from most booksellers, stationers and newsagents.

The River Avon near Salisbury

Index

Entries in italics refer to illustrations